Surrey S
Croydon -
stall story

100 years of market trading

by Vivien Lovett

***Surrey Street - a stall story* is dedicated to my father, for without him many of the stories, especially those about his family, would not have been recorded.**

Front cover: top left - the Royal visit to Surrey Street, November 29th 1994

top right: Surrey Street in the 1960s

bottom left: Surrey Street, 1913

bottom right: Surrey Street in the 1980s

Back cover: from an original oil painting by Bill Lovett

Pen and ink sketches by Bill Lovett. Epilogue 'forget-me-not' sketch by Vivien Lovett.

ISBN 0-9516710-5-7 First published 1995 © Vivien Lovett

FROSTED EARTH
77 RICKMAN HILL
COULSDON
SURREY
CR5 3DT
TEL: (01737) 554869

FROSTED EARTH

Set in 10pt ITC Garamond

Typesetting and design by ***Pollyphonics, Roman Way, Farnham, Surrey GU9 9RF***

Printed by ***Litho Techniques (Kenley) Ltd., 46-50 Godstone Road, Whyteleafe, Surrey CR3 OEA***

Contents

Foreword by HRH Prince Charles, the Prince of Wales

Introduction 6

Walter 7
Church Path, Croydon 7
The root man 9
Seasons on the stall 13
Going Dutch 14
The French (onion) connection 15

Agnes 16
Portraying prosperity 16
Stubbing up 24

Bill, alias 'young Walter' 26
"Young Walter" Lovett 26
A bad day... 33
A good day 33
Empties day 34
Early one morning 34
In search of bargains 37
Load up the barrow 38
A Woodcote nurseryman 39

Up the top 44
Firmly-established 44
Rose's garden 48

The toy stall 52
To be or not to be.. a market trader 52
Toy time 57

Old-established market traders 59
Jaffa Joe 59
The fruit merchant 61
The Harts 63
'Big firm' - the Toohig family 65
Legs Lemon and Tiddler Knowles 69

Street characters 71
Goldie the newspaper man 71
The Phosferene man 71
Ol' Yates, the up-market down-and-out 73
Sarsaparilla man 75

Surrey Street snippets 77

The boxing fraternity 84
Surrey Street champions 84

The federation chairman 89
Mr. Croydon 89

Epilogue 110

❏ Pictures of the Royal visit 92 ❏ About the author 111 ❏ Bibliography 112

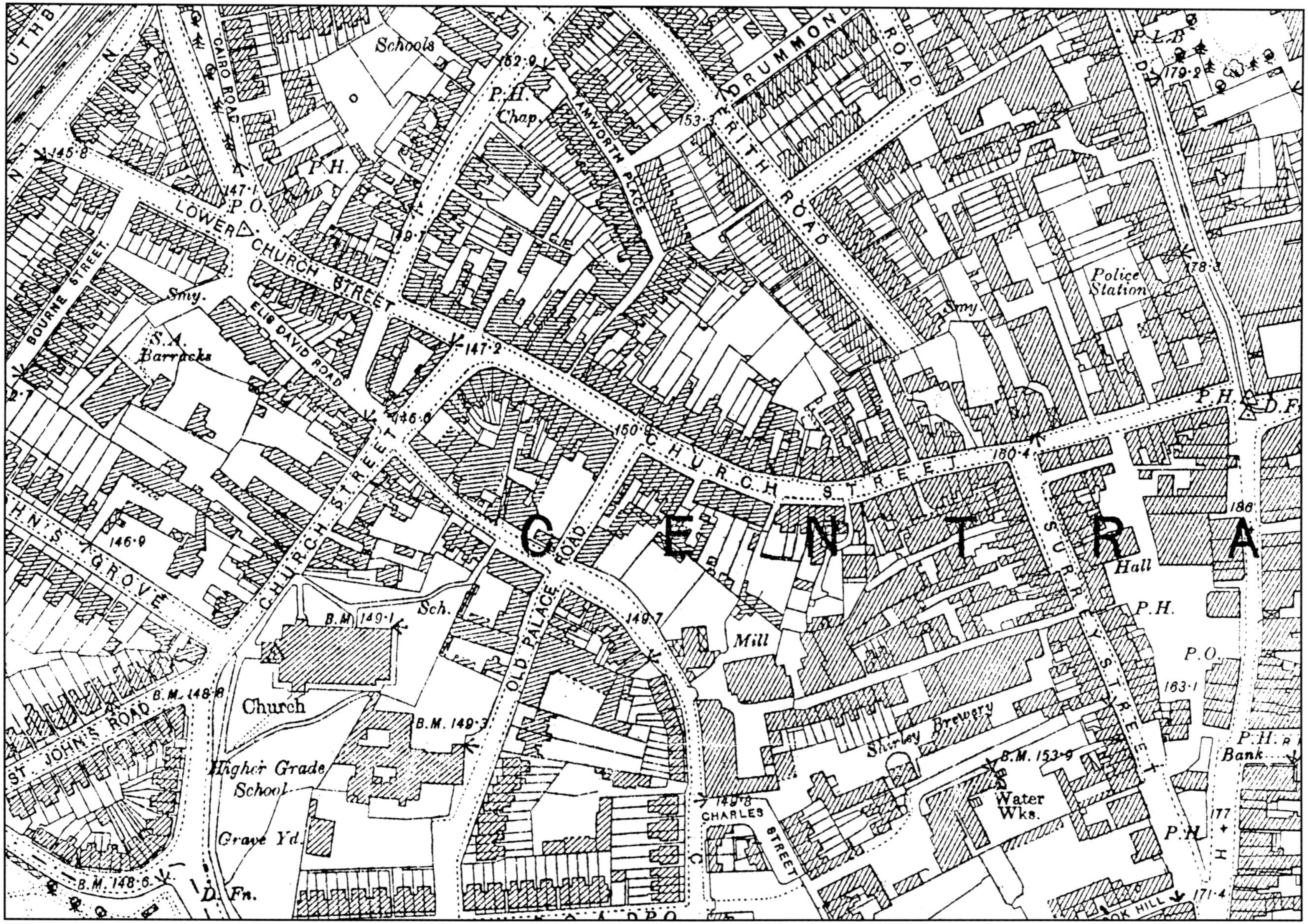

An Ordnance Survey map of 1895. Surrey Street is in the bottom right-hand corner.

ST. JAMES'S PALACE

I am delighted to have the opportunity to provide a short foreword to "A Stall Story". This is not just because I myself spent a most enjoyable morning in Surrey Street last year, during which I had the pleasure of meeting Mrs. Whitehouse but, above all, because I believe quite passionately in the importance of preserving and, frankly, celebrating our unique street markets. They are a particularly colourful part of this country's cultural heritage and it is a cause of great sadness that so many are now under threat because of so-called 'progress'.

I only hope that this splendid little book, describing the history of one family stall, encourages more people to visit Surrey Street, and to appreciate and enjoy the market's vibrancy for themselves.

I am sure the Lovett stall will go from strength to strength in its second hundred years!

Charles

Introduction

"Now only the Surrey Street traders still stand, shouting their wares under an open sky - a living historical monument of the Middle Ages."

Presidential address delivered on March 22nd 1962, by William A. Benians, F.A.I., M.R.S.H., (Trade and Industrial Development of Croydon), from proceedings of the Croydon Natural History and Scientific Society, January - February, 1962.

Croydon Town, as busy today as it has always been, boasts many high-rise office buildings, standing tall and shadowing all below. Somewhere in its concrete undergrowth lies Surrey Street market, little changed in one hundred years and still bustling and bursting at the seams most Saturdays.

The earliest records of the town's market go back to 1276, when Archbishop Kilwardby obtained a Royal Charter for a weekly market, to be held on Wednesdays. It is likely, however, that a market existed before this date, but the charter enabled the collection of taxes and granted the right to hold a nine-day fair in May each year. In 1314 Archbishop Reynolds secured a charter for a corn and cattle market, which was held on Thursdays and in 1343 Archbishop Stratford acquired a grant for a Saturday market which supplied corn and "all kinds of provisions."

The charters also covered the Walnut Fair, which was held in October and the Cherry Fair, which was held in July. The latter is believed to have taken place in the 'triangle,' an area once formed by Surrey Street, Crown Hill and the High Street. This was formerly the site of Croydon's markets.

Over the centuries, with the population increasing, permanent buildings appeared, many being run as boarding houses, most of which, by the late 19th century, were demolished to make way for new buildings.

The former maze of narrow alleyways and streets has now almost vanished.

Surrey Street originally operated as a one-day-a-week market. It has had a succession of names, such as The Shambles, The Flesh Market, The Butcherie and more commonly, Butcher Row. Local residents wanted the name changed, although the reason is not clear. The change was mainly due to the late Benjamin Bean who, before he occupied the prestigious Croydon coaching inn called The Greyhound, had a business in Surrey Street. Dating the market in the street itself is not easy, because licences were not issued in those days, but extracts from an article in the *Croydon Advertiser* of 1894 may throw some light on the market's origins:

"FLOWER MARKET FOR CROYDON:

I think the time has arrived for the Corporation to do something towards the establishment of a public market, especially with regard to the sale of fruit, flowers and vegetables."

The writer went on to say: "Surrey Street has now become a market place for butter, cheese, bacon and a multiplicity of other articles of household use."

It seems likely that once the demolition of the triangle was completed, by 1893, and the re-devel-

Agnes Lovett, pictured in March 1951, celebrating 54 years of trading, when she was 72 years old.

opment programme was complete, the stalls filtered their way into Surrey Street. The 1894 article identified a need for a public market place, so it is probable that the stalls became established shortly afterwards. Surrey Street operated as a daily market from June 1922 and was licensed in 1926, along with many other street markets.

An aunt told me that my very first steps as a child were taken at the 'top end' of the street, on the steps, near Milletts. I now retrace the steps, not mine, but those of my grandparents, who set up their stall in the street in the latter part of the 19th century.

The Lovett stall is the oldest still trading in Surrey Street and by 1997 we hope to be celebrating a century of trading.

It was the discovery of a newspaper cutting (from which the picture on the facing page is taken) of my grandmother, Agnes Lovett, which made me realize that the hundred year mark was imminent.

Surrey Street - a stall story is not a tall story! Through interviews with current and ex-stallholders and relatives, I have managed to peep into the past of this area of Croydon, to relate stories about the daily lives of a few old and well-established traders in Surrey Street from the early part of this century.

Danger at a Christmas party

Walter

Church Path, Croydon

The house is not there any more. The ground on which it once stood is now derelict, lying behind new wooden fencing.

Large mesh gates bar the opening where, once, my grandparents' market stalls would have passed through, to be stored away up in their yard each evening. The entrance is now blocked by builders' rubble and the site is not a pretty one. There was a time, once, when a little community existed here. Small, established firms also traded in this tiny cul-de-sac, where my grandparents, Walter and Agnes Lovett, lived.

In the view from Keeley Road there were six terraced houses on the right-hand side of the street, dating back to around the 1860s. Three houses stood on either side of a bricked archway. My grandparents' house was the first on the right-hand side of the archway.

It looked fairly small from outside, but in reality was surprisingly spacious inside, because of the extra rooms over the archway, with one large room at the front and another at the back.

There was a total of eight rooms. The rooms over the archway were large enough to entertain on a fairly grand scale and my parents would have as many as 30 or 40 people at Christmas functions in this room. At one of these parties, my father,

Walter Lovett (1876 -1948) and Agnes Lovett (1880 - 1954). The couple are pictured here in 1916.

Billy, and his brother, Herbie, had gone outside, for some fresh air and had noticed that the archway floor was vibrating alarmingly under the stress of so many people. Upon my uncle's suggestion, they decided to drive the big trade van under the archway and leave it there for the

Church Path viewed from Keeley Road, looking towards North End, in November 1959.

remainder of the night, just in case the floor should give way and deposit party-goers into the street below.

Through the passageway was a triangular view of the yard, which stretched back quite a depth and afforded generous space for storage. At the very back of the plot, to the left,were the 18th century stables, with huge lofts above, which were originally used by the Rising Sun public house, which was situated behind, in North End. When horse and carriage disappeared and the stables were no longer of any use, the Rising Sun's

Left of picture: rear view of archway and room above. Right of picture: rear of 9, Church Path, Jack and Betty Garcia's house.

My grandparents' house, at 8, Church Path, Croydon. "The front room, over the archway, was the best parlour room."

proprietor discarded them, so the family took them over, to house Walter's plants.

Walter also had a garage, which served as accommodation for his beloved Armstrong Siddeley motor car and ample space outside for storage of their two stalls, trade vehicle and all the produce.

Church Path was also an ideal playground for the children living there. It brought in the children from the Tamworth Road tenements, because it was a quiet, safe place to play rounders, cricket and many other games.

Being a cul-de-sac contributed to this safety factor, but a further benefit came from the absence of cars - very few people could afford a car at that time.

Exotic plants arrive from abroad

The root man

Pre-war years

Walter Lovett c.1920s.

William (Walter's brother) and Edith Lovett in the 1920s.

Jim Lovett, c.1914.

Walter Lovett was only 21 years of age when he fought, at least on one occasion, for his pitch in Surrey Street. The year was 1897.

His father had been a master greengrocer and, although not wealthy, probably helped Walter, and his three younger brothers and sister, to establish themselves in similar trades. Jim, the youngest, worked as a head groundsman at a South East London bowling and tennis club and the others had businesses in Holmesdale Road, Thornton Heath.

Chris had his own fruit and vegetable shop and also managed a local round, using a horse and cart. William had a greengrocer's shop and the only daughter, Martha, and her husband, ran a hardware store, which was eventually altered into

Chris Lovett's children, c.1905.

Agnes and Walter Lovett standing behind their trestle stall in Surrey Street, 1913.

a dairy shop, with a milk round. The milk was delivered using a three-wheeled pushcart.

Before Walter met Agnes he travelled around Croydon and many other towns with his pony and cart, calling at the big hotels and larger public houses, selling palms and ferns, which were fashionable in those later years of Queen Victoria's reign.

My father remembers his mother, Agnes, showing him a miniature horse and cart, with a man holding the reigns; displayed in the cart were tiny potted ferns. She had bought this small ornament because it reminded her of Walter and how he once traded. She even used to sing a song while dusting it: "Three pots a shilling."

That was how much he used to charge for the small ferns.

Walter established himself in Surrey Street in the one-day-a-week market and also traded at his shop in Sydenham Road, Thornton Heath. He rented two shops on separate occasions. The first he called "The Little Marvel" because, he said, it was a marvellous little shop. He later moved to a store opposite, in Dagnall Park.

At the turn of the century, Walter was married to Agnes. Luckily for the Lovett family, the 'top end' (south end of Surrey Street) was the more photographed side - in the accompanying picture, my grandparents and their stall can be seen. In

Martha and her husband, Alfred Foster - c.1900.

Walter's cousins c.1900.

the first few years of market trading, Walter's shops supplied fruit and vegetables. Serving from shop and stall and also delivering to customers for miles around, it was not long before he realized that he would have to change his 'line' if he was to survive in the market place, which at that time was renowned for fruit and veg., so he became a 'root man,' supplying rare and unusual plants that had been brought into Britain by Victorian era botanists.

These plants were being discovered in far-away places, such as China, India and Japan and were being propagated by the specialist nurserymen in and around the London area for the horticultural trade. Such plants are now quite common, but they were rare at the turn of the century. One collector was Ernest Henry Wilson. Born in 1876, he was a Kew-trained man who went to China and discovered the pocket handkerchief tree, *Davidia involucrata,* the jasmine, the virginia creeper and many others.

The *Lilium regale*, the regal lily, almost cost him his life. He arrived in China, which was rife

More of the Lovett 'clan' c.1910.

Dorothy Foster, c.early 1920s.

with small revolutions and uprisings at the time, in 1899. The terrain was treacherous and he had to scale sheer cliff-faces and traverse flooded rivers, to collect rare species. At one stage, he was caught in a landslip which nearly proved fatal.

George Forrest was another such botanist/collector. Born in 1873, he worked for the Royal Botanic Gardens in Edinburgh. It was there that he met the great horticulturalist, Arthur Kilpin Bulley, and the chance arose to go to China as a collector, where he discovered numerous rhododendrons, clematis, hydrangeas and potentillas, to name but a few. These are all well-known plants today. Forrest, too, very nearly lost his life. He was based near the Mekong River, close to the borders of China, India and Tibet. Political and military conditions were volatile in the area in 1905 and he experienced weeks of exhaustion and starvation, with many attempts being made on his life, after being caught up in local uprisings and feuds. Some of Forrest's party met with horrific deaths, being either hacked to pieces or killed by poison arrows. Only one of his party of 17 collectors survived.

There were many other botanists, of course, and my grandfather was to supply numerous rare plants that were introduced by these and other collectors. A few, such as the Himalayan vivid blue poppy, *Meconopsis baileyi*, which Walter sold in the early years, can even today only be obtained from specialist nurserymen.

Some of these plants were expensive. A dwarf alpine plant could cost as much as half-a-crown (12½p), which was a large sum of money in those days, if one considers that the average rent was about 7/6d (37 ½p) in the 1920s.

Walter was supplying plants such as these to his customers who were, in those early years, of the middle and upper classes. They lived in large houses and mansions, which hugged Croydon town. These impressive dwellings had large acreages of land, which needed the skills of gardeners and they were given generous funds to purchase these fashionable and expensive plants.

Walter had his regular customers. My father remembers that, in the 1930s, one such customer, who had a spacious property in Shirley, would come to the stall, put his arm around Walter's shoulder and say: "Send the lot up - I've the gardener coming tomorrow," and would buy the entire show off the stall that day. My father was then told to write down exactly everything that was sold to this customer, go to Covent Garden the next morning, buy a duplicate load, deliver it on his return journey to the customer in question and then drive around the other suppliers and buy what was available, to supplement what was sold on the previous day.

At times my father was followed by some of the 'opposition' from Surrey Street, to find out where he obtained our more unusual stock of plants.

He would recognize their vans and upon his father's suggestion, would 'dodge' them. This practice was quite common, according to other stallholders.

Walter's vehicle before conversion to its trading identity, above, and afterwards, below, c. 1930s.

From left to right: Walter Lovett, Carrie Attrell and Billy Driscoll, trading in close harmony in Surrey Street in the late 1930s.

Martha and Alfred Foster, with their daughter Dorothy, awaiting customers outside their hardware shop in Holmesdale Road, c.1920.

The 1930s

Seasons on the stall

CHRISTMAS was a time when Walter would sell potted plants, such as azaleas, cyclamen and house plants, Christmas trees, wreaths and crosses.

January and February were quiet months, with no real trade for a plantsman. Walter would buy barrels of apples called 'winesaps,' which were grown in Canada, from Covent Garden. Trade was bad on the stall, so Walter and his sons would go out 'calling.'

This meant driving the van around places such as West Wickham, Coney Hall (a favourite place), on estate roads about three miles long, knocking on every door in the road and showing produce. The articles for sale could have been the apples from Canada or cauliflowers, or anything edible, which had been bought at Covent Garden earlier that day. Each item would be sold at half the price charged in the local shops.

March was the start of the hard root season, which consisted of perennials and biennials such as pansies, Sweet Williams and Canterbury Bells. Walter would carry on with these until about the middle of April, when the bedding plant season started. All these he would acquire locally, from nurseries, and this trade would continue until the end of June. April, May and June were extremely

Carrie Attrell's stall, left, and Walter's stall, piled high with plants. The author's father, Bill, is in the background and Aunt Nellie is on the far right. Walter always insisted they stand well back from the stall to let customers have a clear view of the plants.

busy months.

Opposite The Goat public house, in Mitcham, Walter had a plot of rented land and there he grew many hardy perennials himself, especially wallflowers, in the autumn. In those early days the land was dug manually and this task had to be performed every year, so Walter would gather together his labourers, who consisted mainly of 'down-and-outs,' most of them from Surrey Street, such as 'Ol' Yates and his mates.' Walter would take them to the land, where they would dig all day long. He would pay for their lunch, which consisted of huge chunks of bread, cheese and onion, washed down with pints of ale from The Goat.

July and August were very slack months so, having a good plant season, the order of the day was 'enjoy yourself.' Days were spent out at the Sandown Park races, on trips to the coast and general holiday time.

From the end of August, wallflower plants, daffodils and hyacinths and other popular varieties arrived from the Dutch nurseries and were put on sale, right up until Christmas.

Walter Lovett at his stall c.mid-1930s.

1930s onwards

Going Dutch

My grandfather, as well as selling rare and unusual plants, also traded in bulbs and tuberous plants.

One supplier was a Mr. Van der Vis, from Holland. He would invite my grandparents to stay at his home for a week at a time on his shrub nursery near Boskoop. They would walk around, ordering their trees, fruit and ornamental shrubs. Some trees were box varieties, shaped into birds, cockerels, balls and squares, in fact all forms of topiary. These would then be shipped over to the London docks in huge wooden crates.

My father, or his brothers and my grandfather, would pick them up in the truck, making perhaps four or five trips to get them back to Church Path, where they were unpacked and 'stood out' -left in the open air- otherwise the leaves would turn yellow, after being meticulously packed in straw, enclosed in boxes and sealed with rubber straps. Bulbs - hyacinths, crocuses and tulips - were bought in the same way, but from a different supplier.

It seems incredible that a market trader could have dealt in such a way, but it was so with my grandfather. His business was very successful. He used to take the time and trouble to collect the best from each nursery.

He had the finest collection of alpines and perennial plants that one could find. Walter also had his 'imitators,' but at that time he could not be matched for the rare and unusual plants he sold.

Employees lived in the stable lofts

The French (onion) connection

In the early 1930s, Walter and Agnes rented out some of their accommodation in Church Path to Francis and Marie and their entourage. They were French onion-sellers who came to England every year, from around September, to Christmas, to sell their crop of onions, which they grew on their farmland in Roscoff, Brittany.

Francis and Marie rented the 'parlour' inside my grandparents' house, whilst the employees were housed in the stable lofts outside the yard. This was far cheaper than renting other local accommodation, with the 'plus' that the Frenchmen had ample storage space to keep their numerous bags of onions and heavy duty bicycles, which were needed for their rounds.

The lodgings did not include meals. There were plenty of places to eat out, with lots of 'dining rooms,' containing marble-topped tables, where one could buy a large meal of meat and two veg., for a very small charge.

The onions were shipped over every year, to Southampton and delivered by rail and road to Church Path and then stored in the dry lofts above the stables.

The Frenchmen would have their own rounds to such places as Park Hill Rise, Croham Road and Upper Addiscombe Road, Shirley, mainly to middle and upper class residents. This trade was best as the upper classes bought by the 'string,' whereas in the poorer areas people lived from day-to-day and bought loose and cheaply, from the market places.

Whilst the onion sellers went about their business, Marie would stay behind in the stables in Church Path, to string the onions together for the next day's sale. This was done with straw-coloured bass or raffia (a form of natural fibrous material which looked like dried grass, but was much stronger). The modern equivalent of bass is 'nutscene twine.' The bass could also be bought on strands and in various lengths. The onions were linked together in threes, so that one could pull one out from anywhere on the string, without the others falling out. My father said that once these onions were tied up in an airy and cool place, they would keep for many months.

The bicycles were very robust machines, with thick tyres, to enable the Frenchmen to transport the heavy loads of onions for the day's sale. These would be hung over the handlebars, perhaps as many as 20 to 30 strings, amounting to maybe half a day's sale. They would then return to Church Path to replenish their load. The Frenchmen built up a good reputation and had the same rounds every year.

At the outbreak of the Second World War Francis was called up to serve in the French Army and had to return home, as did his labourers. Nothing was heard of them throughout the war. Francis reappeared in peacetime but did not take up his former occupancy of the stable lofts, because these were then being used to house Walter's nursery stocks. Francis used to visit the stall and Church Path however, but was now working 'solo,' selling onions once again, but this time using a three-wheeled van.

The pre-war years

Agnes Lovett, c.1920s.

Agnes

Portraying prosperity

Monty, the family dog, painted by Plummy, c.1935, using a shaving brush!

Walter ('Plummy') Lovett -the eldest son- c.1916.

Agnes was only 18 years old when she married Walter. They spent their honeymoon at the Victoria Coffee Tavern, now part of Reeve's furniture storerooms, at the bottom of Lower Church Street. Taverns, which were little different from bed and breakfast accommodation today, would also have been used as lodging houses.

My grandmother had been a petite woman, only five feet tall, if that, and slim in figure when young, but she became rather plump during her middle years, because by this time she had given birth to 13 children, of which ten were to survive.

Not only did Walter fight for his pitch in Surrey Street, but Agnes also assisted - by hitting other market traders with her handbag!

Agnes told one of her grand-daughters that after two weeks of this type of onslaught, the other market traders no longer found the contested pitch desirable. She helped on the stall at every opportunity. Her personality suited the trade and she was a good saleswoman.

Always immaculately dressed, she hated getting her coat dirty and when serving would wear a pure white overall, which she changed daily (see picture on right).

Agnes was always smiling, pleasant and polite

Young Billy and Agnes Lovett in her pure white working overall, c.mid-1930s.

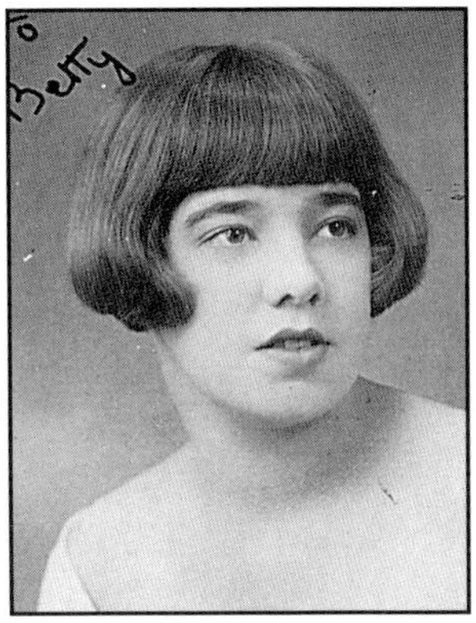

Dorothy (Dolly) Lovett - c.1938.

Elizabeth (Betty or Bebe) Lovett- c.1915.

Kathleen (Kath) Lovett - c.1920

Violet Lovett-eldest daughter- 1932.

Albert (Bert) Lovett - 1938.

Marie (Pam or Pansy) Lovett - c.mid 1930s.

Helen (Nellie) Lovett - 1938.

Herbert (Herbie) Lovett - 1942.

Middle of front row: Dolly Lovett and to the right, Walter and Agnes, going away to Jersey, mid 1920s. The close-up picture of Walter and Agnes on page 22 is taken from this photograph.

in her manner to her customers. She was an optimistic person with a happy-go-lucky attitude and was constantly chatting.

My father told me that it used to take her hours to get home from the market stall in Surrey Street to Church Path, which would normally have taken only a few minutes, owing to her numerous stops on the way, nattering to this person or that. She was hardly ever at a loss for words, which my grandfather took in good part as he had rather a quiet, unhurried manner. Agnes would often remark about him: "If the house was on fire he'd still stop to do up his bootlaces."

She had some curious sayings, such as: "You giddy old whelk, you," or, upon reprimanding her offspring: "I've told you two or three times once before," or, when driving to the coast in the Armstrong Siddeley: "It's all uphill, going down, isn't it, Walter?"

As well as serving on the stall, she had another little business on the side. People used to come to her, mainly on the stall and sell rings, cameo brooches or pawn tickets to her, if they were hard up. The latter she would exchange for the items on them at Bowman's Jewellers, West Croydon, after paying what was due. She was extremely knowledgeable about gems, gold and antiques. She loved brass and had numerous candlesticks

Betty and Doreen Fitzall, wearing the berets brought back for them from France by their grandparents, Walter and Agnes, c. late 1920s.

David William (Bill) Lovett, the youngest son, in 1941.

on the mantelpiece.

She always seemed to have money and hid it in different places around the house. In those days working class people did not trust banks and kept their cash in all sorts of odd places. Agnes was no exception and her favourite place for concealment of cash was her knitting bag. When times were hard, usually during winter periods, Walter would remark: "Don't know how we're going to manage this week, Aggie." She would then produce a roll of banknotes which she had saved and hidden in the more prosperous summer months.

Agnes and Walter earned a good living off the stall in their day. They worked hard and because their business was a success they lived very well, with annual visits to Holland for bulb purchasing, trips to France and they thought nothing of popping down to Devon or Cornwall for a break in the summer months.

Before my father was born, in 1921, my grandparents would travel around by means of a pony and trap. Walter and Agnes loved animals and would never use a whip on Old Tom, the pony, but instead Walter would gently throw a handful of sand, from a tin he kept close by, or soil from the plant root boxes, to make him 'trot on.'

Old Tom was a docile creature, who was also useful to the younger members of the family when playing shops in Church Path yard. Pam,

Dolly Lovett, top right, with the Victoria Girls, at the Victoria Theatre, London, c.mid-1930s.

Nellie and Bert used Old Tom as a counter. They would get him to lay on his side on the ground and there he would stay whilst they played on him with their cardboard money. Occasionally Old Tom would lift his head and one of the children would say: "Lay back down, Tom, we're still playing our game."

The pony would lower his head again and wait patiently for the game to finish.

Walter Lovett in his Armstrong Siddeley, c. mid-1930s

When my father was about six years old, Walter acquired a brand new Model-T Ford, which was known as the Tin Lizzie, and was the first mass-produced motor car.

It was supposedly well-known among Croydon's car dealers that the Lovetts were the first family in town to own this model of car. My grandparents were very 'modern' for their time. They had the money to purchase the latest commodity and as Walter's nephew worked for Dees of Croydon at that time, he would have had instant knowledge of the availability of such a vehicle.

By the early 1930s, Walter owned the Armstrong Siddeley, a wonderful car: "As smooth as silk, which used to glide along," my father recalled. It had a preselector gearbox and a sphinx mascot on the radiator.

As to the acquisition of the Armstrong Siddeley, my father can only guess that it was probably bought from a customer whose husband had died. At that time, women seldom drove.

Agnes had one real extravagance - her hats. She would spend what was then an absolute fortune on them. To another working class person it must have seemed immoral to squander as much as £20 or £30 buying a new hat each year.

In the 1930s, wages would have been around £2.10s (£2.50) per week. These hats were worn on outings to the races, at Ascot and Epsom. She owned hats with feathers, others with flowers; a veil on another. She had a large bird of paradise type which would have been very expensive, being rare in those days. A 'casino chapeau in black velour plush, with real cross-osprey' was priced at 11 guineas (£11.11s - or in modern terms £11.55).

She also had a passion for rings and gold bracelets. Agnes owned a crocodile-skin handbag which was always full of jewellery, sovereign and charm bracelets, a crocodile tooth necklace, and an ivory tusk brooch shaped like an Indian dagger, with necklaces and earrings to match.

Agnes Lovett, with possibly, her first-born child, c. 1900.

Left to right: Kath, Agnes and Mrs. Bloomfield, a friend, on a seaside outing c.1930s.

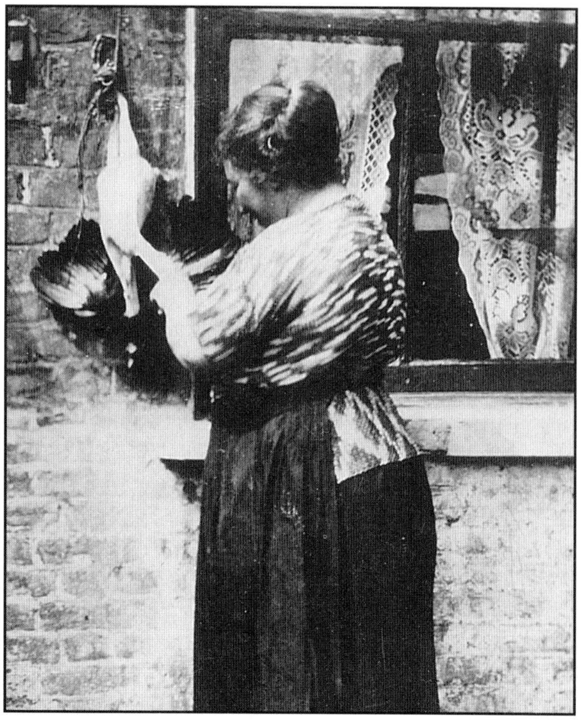

Agnes Lovett, at Church Path, probably in the 1920s, preparing dinner.

From left to right: Elizabeth (Betty or Bebe) Lovett, who was a Pony Girl at the Victoria Theatre, Agnes and Dolly, dressed for dancing classes at The Selhurst School of Dancing, Addiscombe, c. 1920s.

She did not believe in just keeping these for her personal use, however, and knew they would have retained their value and were kept as an investment to see herself and Walter through lean periods. The couple were always immaculately dressed and their success as market traders showed.

They loved dressing up to go up to London on their half-day off (Wednesdays), driving 'up town' in the Armstrong to Monicadams tea rooms for the afternoon and then on to the theatre or vaudeville (music hall) in the evening, especially the

A view of the 'chorus line' at the Victoria Theatre, showing Dolly Lovett, far right, c. mid-1930s.

Victoria Theatre, to see their daughters, Dolly and Betty. They were dancers at the theatre, a venue which featured stars such as the Crazy Gang, Arthur Prince, Max Miller and many others.

Their nephew, Leon Garcia also featured at the Theatre Royal, Drury Lane, in the long-running stage show South Pacific.

Agnes was a very homely person, as well as a good saleswoman and her house was immaculate. Nobody ventured into the kitchen on Monday mornings, her washdays. Her hands and arms would be immersed in bubbles, washing all the 'delicates.'

In the winter months there was always an inviting fire to sit by and one year the family were able to obtain an extra supply of wood, when workmen resurfaced Church Path road. Under the original tarmac lay a surface of wooden blocks and all the occupants in Church Path were offered them as firewood.

The only problem was that they became lethal weapons, because small stones from the road surface had become embedded in the wooden blocks, so once they started to burn, the stones spat out all round the room, making what should have been a relaxing evening by the fire a hazardous experience.

Walter and Agnes Lovett enjoying the good life, c. mid-1920s.

A stage photograph of Dolly Lovett,1920s.

A stage photograph of Betty Lovett, when she was 18 years old, c.1920s.

Agnes' 'allocations' during and just after the war were another source of income for her.

Her fruit allocations were apples by the barrel, crates of oranges, foreign (winesap) apples, a small amount of foreign pears, all of which, on average, would be shipped every two months.

Just after V.E.Day Agnes received her allocation. My father was home on leave and was asked to take four double crates, containing 350 oranges in each crate, to the stall in Surrey Street. He placed them on his warehouse trolley, with his scales on top and pushed the trolley along Frith Road and up Surrey Street.

A lot of traders were giving my father odd looks as he proceeded towards the top end and he was astonished to find, on looking back, that he had a stream of customers following him all the way up the street.

He never bothered to pack out the stall - he just placed the scales on an orange box and began serving the oranges.

Trading in Surrey Street during the war was very haphazard; the stalls would only be put out when produce was available, with trading lasting only a few hours. All edible produce would be sold out.

Walter Lovett, c. late 1930s.

Walter is in the wheelchair in this picture taken on V.E.Day 1945. Either side of Walter are his two grandchildren, Terry Smith, left, and Leon Garcia, right, in party hats. Miriam is behind Walter, left, as is Agnes (in fur hat) and Betty is on the right.

Before and after the war

Stubbing up - and melting the 78s!

Agnes Lovett in 1951.

Stubbing up was a particular job which Agnes, and the girls of the Lovett family, carried out each year for the Christmas trade. The term referred to the crosses and wreaths which were made in the stables at Church Path, in the weeks preceding Christmas.

It entailed threading berries on to the thin stub wires, twisting them, then placing on to thicker wires, again twisting and bending them until they were secure. Agnes would then weave the wires into the wreaths and crosses which Walter would have previously 'mossed up.'

The wooden frames for the wreaths and crosses were made by my father, beforehand. The frames for the crosses would have been fashioned from roofing slates, the crosses nailed and wired, that way being doubly secure. The wreaths would have been constructed from the wooden hoops taken off grape barrels.

Almeria grapes were a late variety, which came from Spain, and were sold at Christmas time. These barrels were extra 'bunce' for the fruit and vegetable stallholders because they would be sold, in plenty, to Walter, to be used for the wreath-making. The barrels, about two-feet high, were bound together with wooden hoops, the top, middle and bottom of the barrel being secured with three hoops in each section. Nine individual hoops were produced from each barrel and were used for 'mossing up' by Walter, who layered moss, entwined with string, around the frames. Agnes would then decorate them with holly leaves, bereft of berries, overlapping the leaves until the moss was completely covered. Then she wired in the berries, called 'nobs,' just four or five per wreath.

Before the Second World War, Agnes would have chosen the ceramicware for her Christmas bulbs, on her annual visit to Holland. Wishing wells, logs, boots, windmills and Dutch girls with buckets would have been sent from Holland to England, by boat, and then delivered to Church Path. Agnes would fill the containers with heathers, dwarf tulips, crocuses and miniature ivies. She sold tiny black boots with laces and inside each boot would be a 'tot' - a very small pot in which Agnes planted white heathers. They looked very effective, black against white.

After the war, when pottery was scarce, my father had the idea of making plant containers out of the logs which the family normally sold for people's fires, when the plant season was quiet. He would hand-saw the sides and ends off these logs and nail them together, making a hollowed log. The remainder of the original log could then still be sold, but was much reduced in size after this onslaught. Again Agnes would plant dwarf tulips and heathers and the logs would be put on sale for the Christmas trade.

The family also had the smart idea of melting down 78 r.p.m. records.

These would be put in the oven, heated through so as to be malleable, removed from the heat and then shaped into 'art deco' handkerchief bowls, while still warm.

Agnes was heartbroken when Walter died in 1948, at the age of 71 years. They had been devoted to one another. She made him a six-foot high white cross with white carnations and inserted red carnations through the middle to give the appearance of the cross bleeding.

One of the daughters made a heart-shaped wreath, again with red carnations breaking through the heart, and all the grandchildren had a flower each to put on Walter's coffin. Three open-backed lorries, full of wreaths, came from Covent Garden and the Surrey Street traders made a huge procession and attended his funeral. It was the end of an era; the end of a man who had found his niche in Surrey Street.

Agnes died in 1954. Her funeral was not quite as large, remembering that Walter had still had most of his contemporaries around him. They had virtually all disappeared when Agnes passed away, at the age of 74 years.

Walter and Agnes are now re-united and are buried at Croydon Cemetery, in Mitcham Road.

Leon and Betty Garcia at work in Church Path yard in the mid-1950s.

Early years at the market

Young Walter Lovett

...or Bill, alias 'young Walter'

My father was born in 1921, on Walter's 46th birthday. Agnes was 42 years old and the new baby, the thirteenth child, was the last that Walter and Agnes were to have. It was also on Walter's exact birthday that Surrey Street received a visit from His Royal Highness the Prince of Wales, on November 29th 1994. The first stop which the Prince made was also, coincidentally, at Walter's stall.

My father had accompanied Walter on his business trips, when quite a young lad and, although christened David William, and nicknamed Billy, or Bill, he was always addressed as "young Walter" by the Covent Garden suppliers, cart minders and other traders, when he travelled with Walter. My father also helped out in his school lunch-times, with bike at the ready, to deliver Walter's plant orders. One day Walter sent him off down the Brighton Road saying: "It's just down the Brighton Road, Billy, it won't take you long." My father finished up in Redhill - it was still the Brighton Road. Needless to say he was late for afternoon classes.

In the 1930s, Saturday trading continued well into the evening, perhaps as late as ten o'clock. For my father, being quite young, it was a very long day, if one remembers that Walter and son would have left Church Path at around 4am that morning to go to Covent Garden for the day's purchases. At the end of the evening, before returning home to Church Path, Walter and Agnes would sometimes walk from their stall in Surrey Street and go over the road to the Green Dragon public house, for a nightcap.

My father, when he was about 12 years old, remembers waiting outside the Green Dragon for Agnes to bring him out a Brighton biscuit - a huge shortcake biscuit - and a bottle of fizzy lemonade. These he took back to the stall.

On that occasion, his appetite appeased and his thirst quenched, he felt very tired so he climbed up on the empty stall to lie down. He covered himself with a tarpaulin, to keep the night's chill

Bill Lovett in 1924, aged 2½ years.

at bay, and then fell asleep.

Ol' Yates, Walter's helper, arrived to return the stall to Church Path and, being unaware of my father's presence, he pushed the stall down Surrey Street, along Frith Road, and up Church Path.

It was left in the yard where it was stored each night. All this time my father remained sound asleep. A little while later, Walter and Agnes reappeared in Surrey Street and finding that their stall had been returned to Church Path, they made for home. Panic set in, though, when my

Bill Lovett standing at the back door of the family's home in Church Path, Croydon, in 1932.

father could not be found. Agnes thought he had made his own way back, it was only a short distance from Surrey Street to Church Path, but there was no sign of him anywhere. Walter and Agnes set off for the police station whilst the remainder of the family went out and searched for him. Many hours later, in the early hours of the morning, my father woke up feeling very cold. He popped his head out from under the tarpaulin and wondered how on earth he had got to Church Path. Being very surprised at finding himself at home, he jumped off the stall and made his way down to the house, went through the back door and there found all his startled family. Upon hearing of the night's events everyone burst out laughing. It was all taken in good heart.

Although my father was to help Walter with the plant deliveries, he also enjoyed a very happy childhood, taking himself off to the local cinema, which cost him 6d. (2½p), or swimming at the baths in Scarbrook Road, which cost him 2d. (1p).

Home entertainment included listening to the wireless set, which ran on wet batteries, known at the time as 'accumulators,' and hearing big bands such as Henry Hall, Jack Payne and Roy Fox. He also learnt to fight from a very early age, and Agnes had him measured for plus-fours while he was still at school. My father hated these trousers and one can imagine the derision he suffered, not only from his schoolmates but from the teachers as well. He made sure the outfit was worn out fairly quickly so he could be fitted into 'long uns.'

The plus-fours were made by Mr. Glazer, best bespoke, of Jewish denomination, who would walk up and down Surrey Street, occasionally, always with tape measure at the ready. He would measure stallholders on the spot, on the rare occasions when they weren't busy, and have one or two samples of trousers for them to try on, or he would call around to their homes on Sunday mornings to obtain a sale. His shop was situated

Bill's delivery bike - father delivered fruit trees as well as plants.

From left to right, standing: Bill, a family friend, Agnes and Walter; sitting: Betty, with her daughter, Miriam. The photograph was taken at Whitley Bay, near Newcastle, c. 1935.

in Station Road, West Croydon, but if trade was quiet he would go out looking for orders down Surrey Street, and once asked my father: "You want a luverly suit, my boy?"

The years passed by, my father completed his schooling and helped with the family business. Walter and Agnes decided to send him to horticultural college, but when the Second World War broke out he joined the army instead, and was eventually involved with the Normandy landings, at Arromanches.

He was with the 45th Armoured Division, in the 179th Field Regiment. After the battle for Caen, the British and Americans broke through the Falaise Gap, which led to the liberation of the Belsen concentration camp. My father, still only 23, was expected to return home, after a five-year absence, forget the horrors of war and continue life where he had left off.

A letter from my father, (which begins on page 31) sent to his sister in 1944, from Germany, portrays a young man making the best of a bad situation, but another battle was to ensue upon his arrival home. British soil was now occupied, not by the Germans but by every edible crop that could be grown, because of the wartime food shortages. Growers and householders were

Bill, Agnes and Walter Lovett, c. 1933.

restricted from growing flowering plants such as roses or shrubs and this led to shortages in the trade.

Local growers could now take advantage of this and bypass Covent Garden, which had once been my father's main source of supply. Most of the produce which was available at that time included vegetables such as tomatoes, brussels sprouts, cabbage plants and broccoli, and rhubarb. Food shortages were still a real threat, so my father purchased seedlings and grew all these on the plot of land in Mitcham, as well as buying from local suppliers. So this was to be yet another test of survival in Surrey Street. Walter managed to change his line from fruit and vegetables to rare and unusual plants, but for my father to survive he had to revert back to fruit and veg.

In the spring and summer of 1946 my father was supplied with local produce from the few contacts which Agnes had retained during the war. Others had to be sought, because many changes had taken place in the five years since he went away.

It was also a case of 'manufacturing' goods, such as the 'handkerchief' bowls, that the family made, or going into the countryside and buying huge quantities of logs for local sale. One of their trips, when they went to Brighton, proved very successful. A landowner needed to fell many trees in an acre of woodland. Agnes paid £350 for the timber, which also included a saw bench.

Christmas greetings for 1944, with best wishes for 1945, including the wyvern insignia of the 43rd Armoured Division.

Bill Lovett, Royal Corps of Signals, 43rd Armoured Division, in 1944.

Over the next two months, the family sawed thousands of logs which they sold wholesale to Halls, the local builder, and were presented with their first-ever cheque, for the initial payment of £400. Up to that time the family did not have a bank account, so my father took the cheque into a Croydon bank to get it changed.

He was most perturbed when the manager would not comply with his request. My father had no idea how banks operated, having always only dealt in cash. Most people in those days paid that way; rolls of banknotes, secured with rubber bands, is the way I remember my father keeping his cash.

There were no credit cards at that time, either. Obviously larger concerns paid by cheque but most small, individual buyers, like my father, would always pay in cash, but now the time had come for the family to open a bank account. It still amazes my father when he thinks of Agnes and the £350 cash she made available for the

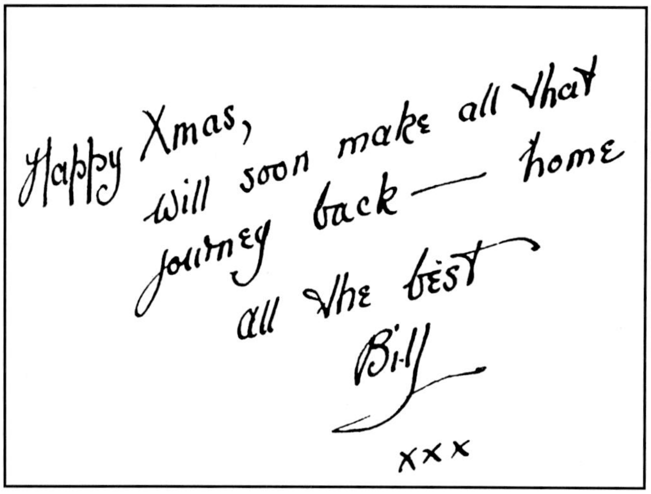

Christmas greetings sent during the war years, from Bill.

wood purchase, in 1946, but perhaps it isn't really so surprising when one remembers why she kept antiques, gold and jewellery hidden away in the house...for those 'lean' periods, of course.

Another piece of luck came my father's way. I say luck, but upon thinking about it, luck is the residue of hard work, not just physically, but mentally as well. It was one of the reasons why I wanted to write my book, to enlighten the public so that they knew a market trader is not all that he or she seems.

Most traders, especially in the early years, were 'entrepreneurs' and the dictionary definition of that word is: "A person who attempts to profit by risk and initiative." My father, like so many, had to take many financial risks. He gambled with a change of line, he gambled with the weather and he gambled in bulk buying.

So another gamble took place, just after the Second World War ended, with Christmas trees. The family bought 'thinnings' from the Forestry Commission. The only difficulty with this land clearance was that the trees had been grown on the side of a hill. At this particular time the Lovetts, and only a few other traders, such as Patsy Toohig, were selling Christmas trees, in Surrey Street. Not only were thousands of trees cut down by the family, but many were literally pulled out of the ground, by hand, to obtain the whole root, because there was a better sale that way.

The problem was, though, that the ground was frozen and on the side of a steep slope, but the frequent tumbles to the bottom of the hill, by my father and his brother, Bert, provided comic relief from the back-breaking labour.

The family cleared thousands of Christmas trees from this particular piece of land at Rusper, in

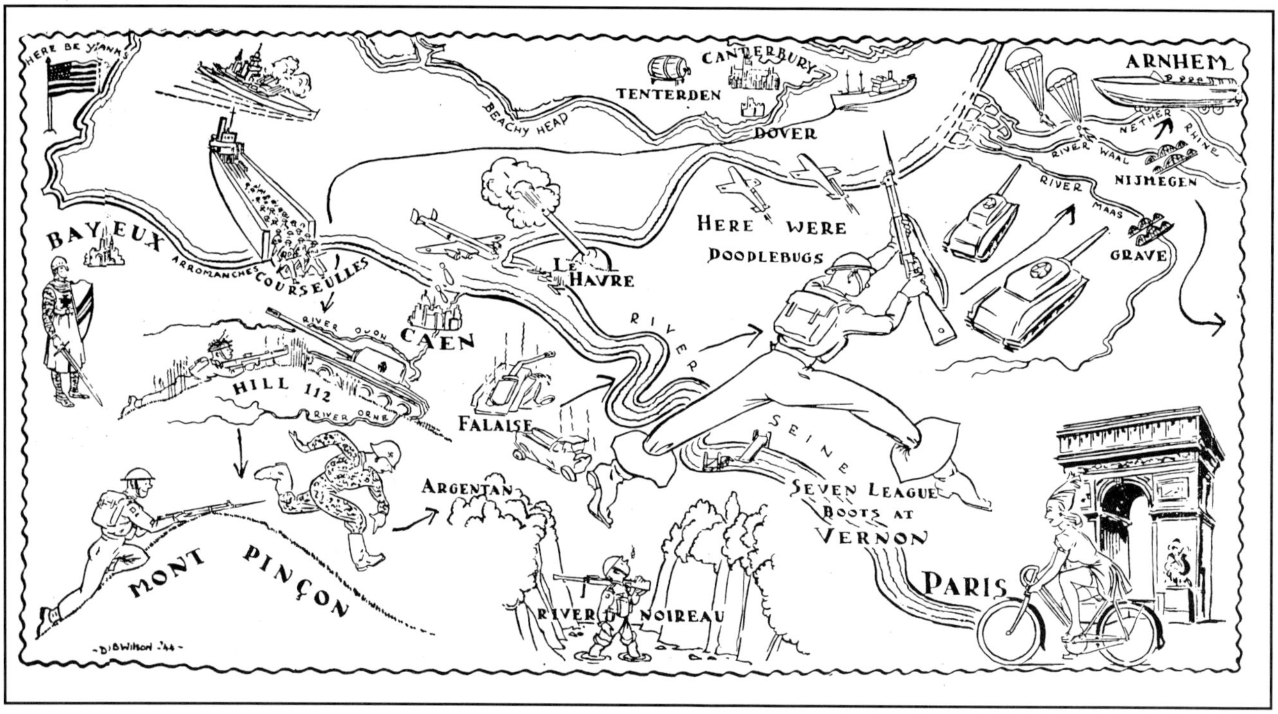

Walter's stalls, in their heyday (1931) in Surrey Street. Walter's helper, George Thorogood, wearing a cap, can be seen in this view. The Thorogoods are another old and established family of traders in the street.

Sussex, and managed to sell most of the trees on a wholesale basis, as well as on the stall in Surrey Street.

Walter, too, was very much the entrepreneur and my father recalled a rather funny incident, which took place while Walter was still alive. It was with regard to Christmas trees, and occurred just before the Second World War. One year in the late 1930s, and just after the festive season, Walter found that he had three Christmas trees, each seven-feet tall, which were unsold.

He mentioned this to my father who said he would take them back to Mitcham and burn them on our plot of land. "No you don't," said Walter, "I'll sell them for New Year." My father thought that Walter had gone quite mad and said: "I'm not selling Christmas trees in the New Year, people will think I've gone crazy." Walter replied: "No, I'll get them sold, you wait and see, plenty of Scots will buy them." Well, they did. The three Christmas trees were sold by midday on New Year's Eve, to three Scots for their Hogmanay celebrations. That was using one's initiative.

By 1946, my father had taken over Walter's stall. His father had suffered a stroke by this time and could no longer help in the family business. My father bought an ex-army, reconditioned lorry, which cost £180.

Now he had transport, although very little money left to purchase produce for the stall. He

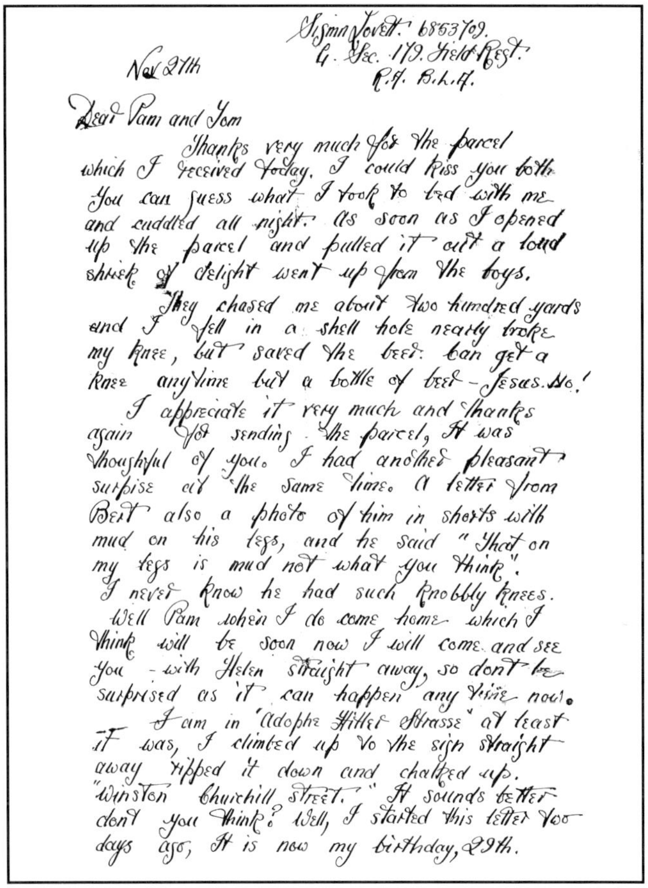

Sigmn Lovett. 6863709.
G. Sec. 179. Field Regt.
R.A. B.L.A.

Nov 27th

Dear Pam and Tom

Thanks very much for the parcel which I received today. I could kiss you both. You can guess what I took to bed with me and cuddled all night. As soon as I opened up the parcel and pulled it out a loud shriek of delight went up from the boys.

They chased me about two hundred yards and I fell in a shell hole nearly broke my knee, but saved the beer. Can get a knee anytime but a bottle of beer - Jesus. No!

I appreciate it very much and thanks again for sending the parcel, it was thoughtful of you. I had another pleasant surprise at the same time. A letter from Bert also a photo of him in shorts with mud on his legs, and he said "That on my legs is mud not what you think". I never knew he had such knobbly knees.

Well Pam when I do come home which I think will be soon now I will come and see you - with Helen straight away, so don't be surprised as it can happen any time now.

I am in 'Adolphe Hitler Strasse' at least it was, I climbed up to the sign straight away ripped it down and chalked up. "Winston Churchill Street." It sounds better don't you think? Well, I started this letter two days ago, it is now my birthday, 29th.

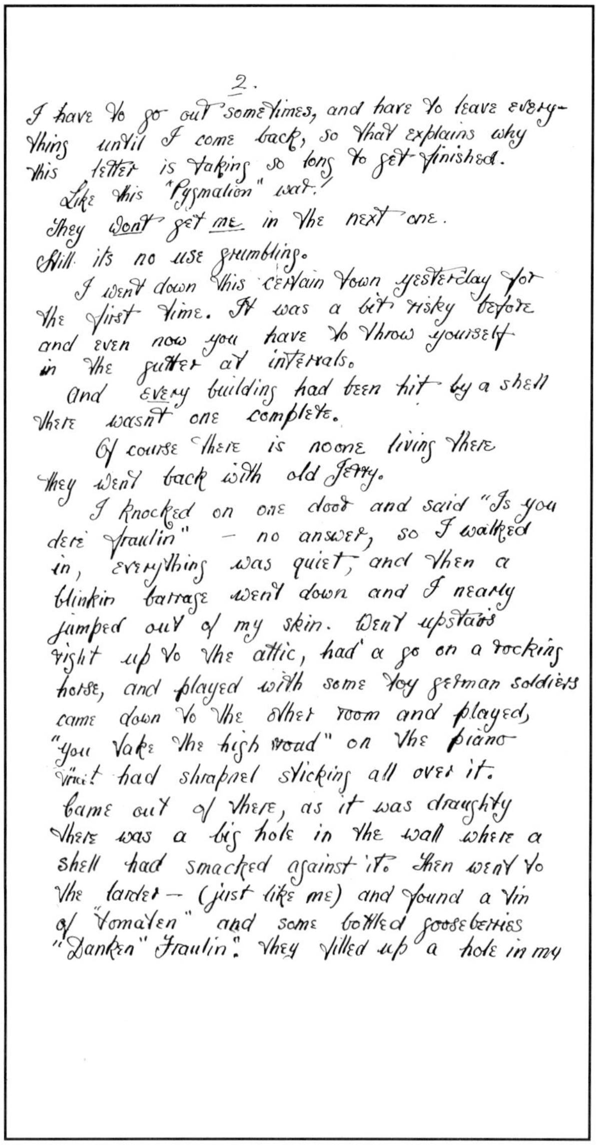

2.

I have to go out sometimes, and have to leave everything until I come back, so that explains why this letter is taking so long to get finished.

Like this "Pygmalion" war.!

They don't get me in the next one.

Still its no use grumbling.

I went down this certain town yesterday for the first time. It was a bit risky before and even now you have to throw yourself in the gutter at intervals.

And every building had been hit by a shell there wasn't one complete.

Of course there is noone living there they went back with old Jerry.

I knocked on one door and said "Is you dere fraulin" – no answer, so I walked in, everything was quiet, and then a blinkin barrage went down and I nearly jumped out of my skin. Went upstairs right up to the attic, had a go on a rocking horse, and played with some toy german soldiers came down to the other room and played, "You take the high road" on the piano that had shrapnel sticking all over it. Came out of there, as it was draughty there was a big hole in the wall where a shell had smacked against it. Then went to the larder – (just like me) and found a tin of "tomaten" and some bottled gooseberries "Danken" fraulin". They filled up a hole in my

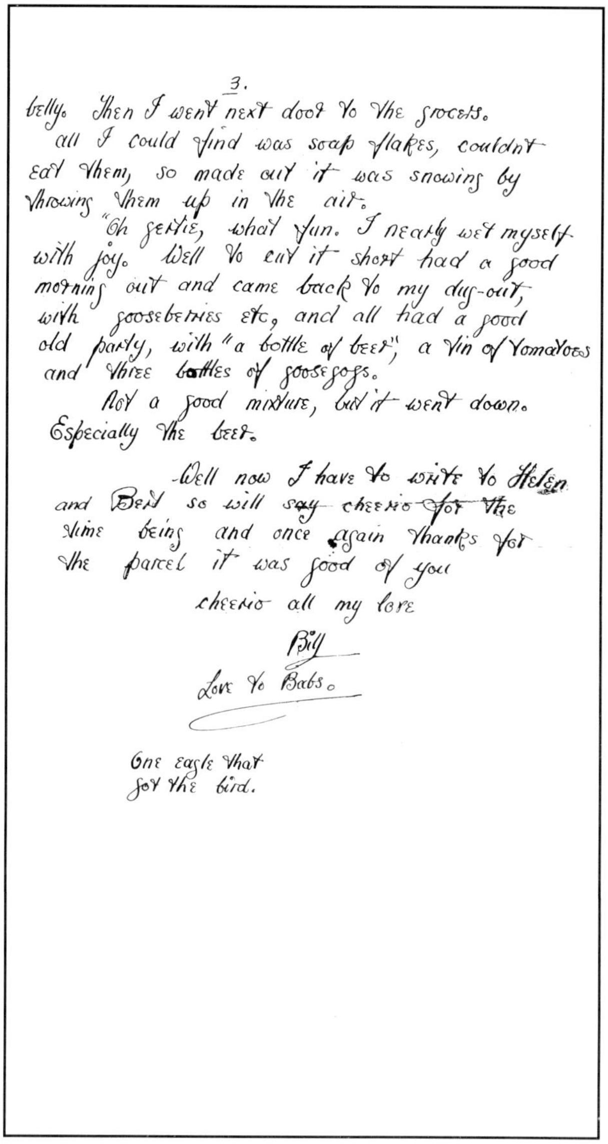

3.

belly. Then I went next door to the grocers. All I could find was soap flakes, couldn't eat them, so made out it was snowing by throwing them up in the air.

"Oh gertie, what fun. I nearly wet myself with joy. Well to cut it short had a good morning out and came back to my dug-out, with gooseberries etc, and all had a good old party, with "a bottle of beer", a tin of tomatoes and three bottles of goosegogs.

Not a good mixture, but it went down. Especially the beer.

Well now I have to write to Helen and Bert so will ~~say~~ cheerio ~~for the~~ the time being and once again thanks for the parcel it was good of you

cheerio all my love

Bill

Love to Babs.

One eagle that got the bird.

The two final pages of a letter from Germany - sent by Bill Lovett in 1944.

therefore bought cheap lines, whatever was available, perhaps pears or plums, and slowly he built the business up and then went back into plants once again.

My father carried on with Walter's line of plants for the next 15 years, but always remembered his father's philosophy in business: "Never be married to anything; if it earns, sell it." This means don't fall in love with any commodity, putting a high price on it.

By around the mid-1950s, more competition came into Surrey Street, so, with history repeating itself again, my father decided it was time to 'change his line.' In previous years my father would not buy cut flowers because they were sold on his neighbouring stall in Surrey Street.

Winnie Conners had been there for many years, and always sold flowers. There was an unwritten costermonger's law that you did not spoil another person's pitch, and Walter certainly obeyed the rules in his day, as had my father.

Once Mrs. Conners had relinquished her stall, however, the coast - and my father's conscience - were both clear.

Ups and downs in the 1950s

A bad day...

Earnings for a market trader are not, and never were, guaranteed. You could have a good week or a very bad one, depending on various factors. The primary one was the weather; obviously rain and snow were certainly classed as resulting in bad days.

My father remembers a very bad day one Christmas. Every year he would purchase 1,000 Christmas trees, These were quite a line to sell as very few traders in Surrey Street sold them in the 1950s.

However, this particular year there was a glut, many being imported, and half the stalls in Surrey Street were selling them. Trade was so bad that stallholders were drastically undercutting one another so that they could, at least, recoup their initial outlay.

This was clearly visible to the public and traders were being offered half the price quoted on their sales tickets.

In those days the average price for a Christmas tree was around 12/6d. (62p), for a tree which was five-to-six-feet tall - but the customers were offering only half that amount. Being desperate, especially at that time of the year, the trader invariably took the offer.

Nobody sold out of Christmas trees in Surrey Street that year. They were left in the alleyways, dustcarts and gutters, on Christmas Eve. People on their way home from work picked up one, or more, for free. My father took his remainder back to our smallholding, along with others from Church Path yard, and, collecting more stock on our land burnt each and every one of them.

We had a monstrosity of a greenhouse boiler which digested one whole Christmas tree at a time. Along with coke to keep the fire bright, my father fed the boiler about 400 trees.

The following year hardly any market traders in Surrey Street bought Christmas trees - and there was a shortage.

...a good day

My father remembers a very good day, back in the 1950s. It was the August Bank Holiday period and the plant season had finished. 'Root men' had to fill in with other lines and my father went to Covent Garden to scour the streets for a cheap line but one which was sufficiently inexpensive as to warrant a queue to form in Surrey Street.

He walked around Covent Garden, at first without any success. Then a friend came up and said to him: "Pop into Pouparts, in the banana-cutting room, and you'll pick up a bargain." This my father did and found the room full of stalks of bananas. Today they come packed in boxes and, although boxed in the past you could also buy them 'on the stalk.' Being August Bank Holiday, Pouparts, large importers at Covent Garden, wanted to be rid of them as they were already ripe and they were expecting another boatload.

My father took a gamble, bought a ton of bananas and drove back to Surrey Street and

Bill Lovett, right, looking for bargains at Covent Garden market, in mid-1946.

parked his van opposite to his stall, at midday on the Friday.

As soon as he bought the stalks over to the stall and cut the bunches, a queue began to form. He sold them at a shilling a pound and undercut the other market traders.

He worked non-stop, on his own, and ran backwards and forwards, cutting and serving. He continued like this until 5pm, by which time he had sold one-third of his cheap stock. Saturday was 'all bunce' - market slang for all profit - and my father worked until 4pm, by which time he had sold out of his bananas. The initial outlay for the ton of bananas was £40 but by Saturday teatime he had £110 in his pocket. Wages, at that time, were around £12 per week.

Returning boxes to the wholesaler

Empties day-1960s

My father used Mondays for collecting his 'empties' around the yard on the smallholding, where we lived.

Unless it was the height of the plant season, Mondays were bad days to 'put out' the stall in Surrey Street.

'Empties' day was very important to a market trader. These were your 'return' boxes to the wholesale markets for which a deposit was kept by the supplier. Boxes were charged at different rates 2s. (10p), 4s. (20p) for half-bushel and bushel baskets. Banana 'coffins' were charged at 10s. (50p) per box in the 1960s. These were long, coffin-shaped wooden boxes which could hold 28lbs of bananas.

The boxes were not of the flimsy material you see today, but much sturdier; their planks measuring as much as a quarter to half-an-inch in thickness. A market trader could amount as much as £50 on an 'empties' day some weeks.

These empties would be taken back to Covent Garden by my father early Tuesday mornings. It was quite a time-consuming task, once there, as he had to go to each individual supplier's 'empty' warehouse to take the returns and collect a token disc for the amount. At the end of returns he would then go to each of the individual supplier's cashiers, to receive his dues.

There were men at Covent Garden called 'empty men' who made a living by taking back your empties for you at a percentage of your returns.

Those trips to Covent Garden

Early one morning

It was back in the 14th century that Covent Garden was once Convent Garden, produce being grown there for the monks of Westminster Abbey. Since the 16th century it has been a trading post and the most famous of fruit and vegetable markets.

It closed on that site, in 1973, and is now situated at Nine Elms, London, a few miles from its original home.

Covent Garden features in a chapter of its own because it was (along with Borough Market and Spitalfields), my father's main source of supply, as it would have been for many market traders.

My grandfather had traded at Covent Garden so my father did the same. Walter had built up a good reputation with his suppliers over the years and this paved the way for my father when Walter had to retire.

Covent Garden was like another world. Once over Waterloo Bridge and into The Strand, the

Covent Garden Market, looking eastward (from a print of 1786).

whole atmosphere changed from the quiet peace of the sleepy suburbs, enjoyed en route from home, into a bustling, thriving market, with street lights ablaze, numerous vehicles and masses of people going about their early morning business.

In the immediate vicinity of the market, the public houses would be open, also cafés, offering morning breakfast. The whole area seemed in complete turmoil.

My father remembers that occasionally he would see the odd night-clubber, a 'Good time Charlie,' and his girlfriend, walking through the market, having been up the West End for the evening, she in her flowing sequined evening dress and he in top hat, bow tie, the works. He would buy her a bunch of flowers, and would still be intoxicated from the wine he had drunk while gambling into the early hours.

The market extended into a maze of streets, with hundreds of small, private concerns winding their way into the gigantic warehouses and out into the streets around. One would never believe that this market, or others, could ever run efficiently and effectively, but my father assures me that they did, although he always called it "a place of organized chaos."

It was divided up into a three-tier system of suppliers. Firstly the small growers who would trade on The Stones around the Piazza; The Stones being the cobblestones which encircled the main market square. No-one else traded here because suppliers were issued with licences for their pitches.

Then there was the wholesale market, small growers who operated inside the building. There were around 100 small-commission agents who used to sell produce for growers. Lastly there were the big importers, such as Pouparts, established in 1895, but the family had been supplying the market from about 1776. There was also Munro's, selling in Covent Garden from around 1862. These were both very big firms although there were others, too. Everything was there, the gigantic warehouses, banana-ripening rooms and cold storage.

The suppliers would arrive many hours before their customers, unloading their produce for the very early morning's sale. My father would arrive at the market at around 4am, perhaps 5am, at the latest, and the first important part of the morning was to find his 'pitch.' This consisted of driving around to his usual pitch which would then be minded by a 'cart minder.' My father would usually go to Wellington Street, where there were a few spaces. His cart minder was a chap called Harry. It was Harry's territory and no other cart

Main market square, Covent Garden, c.1910.

minder would take this territory as it would have been handed down through the family. Each cart minder had his own territory which usually stretched for a whole street for each minder, having between 20-40 vehicle spaces, with a premium of around 2/6d (12½p) each vehicle. A cart minder could earn about £3-£5 per morning, which was a very good income if you consider pre-war wages would have been around £5 per week, on average.

There was one particular time when my father remembers having great difficulty in parking his vehicle in Wellington Street. He arrived extremely late for market one morning. He drove to the end of Wellington Street (which led into The Strand), where a policeman was directing traffic because the lights there had failed. The officer stopped the traffic to let my father pull out; his was the only vehicle, and he turned left to go back into the market again, but he could not find one single space so he had to go back into Wellington Street for a second time, driving to the end and facing the same policeman. The officer scowled at him but stopped the traffic again to let my father out.

A third time round and still nowhere to park. My father faced the same policeman yet again. The officer stood there with his hands on his hips and exclaimed: "If you come around here once more you're nicked." My father wanted to know for what reason and the reply came that he was causing an obstruction! My father assured him that he wasn't, so the policeman, impatiently, waved him on saying he'd just about had enough.

Luckily, for my father, on the fourth time round he found a parking space, for he knew his luck was running out. Bow Street Police Station was literally just up the road!

Once he had parked, in Wellington Street, my father would visit the flower market, buying the miscellaneous produce before it was all sold. He picked out the best and when that job was completed he would visit the specialist growers. These could number as many as four or five, all of whom had reserved plants for him. He never looked for bargains where flowers or plants were concerned, and he never asked the price. The specialist growers would only supply good quality, and unusual varieties. These suppliers would know exactly what my father wanted and would reserve it for him, as they would have done for Walter when he traded with them.

Striving for a living after the war

In search of bargains

Bill Lovett in 1948 listening to a customer - note his 'cheap line' for the day's trading.

When the bedding season came to an end my father had to go fruit-buying in Covent garden. His licence covered plants and fruit. This time he would park in Shelton Street and would see another cart minder, called Darkie, and then he would set off down Long Acre, James Street and Floral Street looking for bargains, and this could entail many miles of walking. He would also look into the Floral Hall, but goodness knows why it was called this, because it was full of fruit!

My father hated this period because picking up bargains was not as easy as it was not his usual trade.

There would be small syndicates, say two or three men, who would get together and buy in bulk, making it difficult for the individual buyer. There were men called 'touts.' These men would never buy or sell anything, but would just go and find inexpensive lines. They would tell friends, people they knew, what bargains could be had. They earned a living doing this. Touts kept to their own contacts, where there was no competition.

If my father couldn't find a bargain he would go along the streets where men earned a living selling on the pavement, but only for fruit and veg. They would wander the market, buying the cheap produce, have them sent out by a porter and then pitch outside a bank or a shop front, somewhere not open.

They would perhaps have as many as 200 packages, or whatever they could purchase. So if my father couldn't find anything he would try and pick up his day's sales this way.

There were many other ways of obtaining bargains. A 'load' could come into Covent Garden late in the day and be 'full on' - meaning ripe - which would then automatically become a bargain. The commissioning agent would want this load sold before the next morning's delivery.

Bargains were at their best in Covent Garden, after the Second World War, because everything had become so disorganized.

Fruit was being sent to England from various continental countries and there was no co-ordination of trading practices. It could, at times, be a market trader's treasure trove. Bargains were produced by the gluts, which occurred when growers sent all they could to any market.

Boatloads of pears, plums or peaches could be bought, and sold, at very low prices. Bargains were nurtured, too, by the absence of mechanical devices to load and unload the produce and street market traders were valued because they would buy in quantity from the wholesalers.

An example of this is when my father spotted a lorry transporting its goods around the narrow thoroughfares into Covent Garden. Its load started to lean, precariously, to one side.

The only way to secure the produce was to drive the lorry next to a lamp-post, so that the goods had something to lean against. This immediately became a 'bargain.' My father was there, bought the pears and had his 'cheap line' for the day's sale.

Porters and porterage

Load up the barrow

Just as Bill Curd (see p.61) would have experienced difficulties at the docks, so my father would encounter problems with porters. Getting his purchases, from all the individual suppliers, back to his vehicle, was not a simple task at Covent Garden, because the lorry might be streets away from where he had been buying.

The floral market was easier. My father would get his own trolley off the vehicle and collect each individual item and take it back, that way, with no porters being involved, even though, in those days, it was possible to hire a freelance porter if you wished.

The fruit market had porters employed by each individual firm. They would charge porterage on each item one bought and would load their barrows to full capacity (keeping their porterage in mind). My father would state where his vehicle was parked and when the porter was free he would deliver the purchases. Sometimes this could be straight away or, if they were extremely busy, my father could wait an hour, or more, for his goods.

This meant interruptions as he would have to walk back to his lorry several times to check whether the goods had been delivered and then to

A traditional costermonger's barrow.

load the lorry himself. This was quite a task after purchasing between 80-100 boxes. Porters were not paid to load vehicles and would throw the goods on to the lorry. This meant that damage could occur so personal attendance was essential.

During the heyday of Covent Garden, porters numbered around 1,000. They pulled everything in those early days and generally it was sheer, physical muscle power that pulled their barrows along. Firms did not have to buy horses, or feed, or stabling, not that any would be found with land being so valuable in town. Manpower was far cheaper. The porters would pull the two-wheeled barrows, which had thick wooden wheels encircled with metal bands to take the wear and tear, and heavy weighted springs to take the load, which could be as much as half-a-ton.

The barrows invariably had a rope across the shafts which could then go round the porter, to give him greater pulling power. Remember that the containers on their barrows would have been sturdy, awkward, heavy boxes and baskets as well as large hessian sacks which contained a hundredweight of potatoes at a time.

The porters, not all of whom were robust-looking - some were small and wiry - would be as strong as carthorses and could pull along the tremendous weights on the barrows, in all weathers. They were on the go all the time. A few of these hand barrows are still used in the wholesale markets today.

After all purchases had been completed, it was time to go and buy the first 'cuppa' of the day. The time was now about 7am.

When my father was a young lad, Walter would take him to a café in Covent Garden, one of many, which was referred to as 'On The Lawn,' and Walter would say to him: "Come along, Billy, we'll go and have tea on the lawn." My father had visions of a café with a lush green lawn at its side, and decked with tables and chairs. Instead he found a café with a narrow serving shelf, no tables or seating and only the pavement for its 'lawn.' An Italian, named Georgio, ran the café and would often call out: "Cuppa tea for the pretty la-adies," and: "wunna roasta beefa san'wicha." Georgio would serve mugs of tea and tell his customers to: "Go, 'avva your cuppa tea onna the lawn." My father's reward would be a giant mug of steaming hot, sweet tea and a huge, thickly-cut roast beef sandwich. This set him up for the rest of the day.

Fish manure gave tomatoes their taste!

A Woodcote nurseryman

It was in 1957 that my father took over a smallholding on Telegraph Track which was on the Little Woodcote Estate, in Wallington. With four acres of land, and starting from scratch, he sowed seeds for growth of statice, marigolds and many other varieties of flowers and plants. He bought approximately 250 chrysanthemum stools - the previous year's plants - from a local nurseryman, and during the autumn planted them into boxes and housed them in the greenhouses over the winter period.

By January or February dozens of cuttings had grown from each stool and these were potted up individually and planted out in spring.

The stools had produced around 10,000 cuttings, which took up about half-an-acre of land and about two months of planting time. With the family's help, and that of my elder brother, David William jnr., who worked for my father upon leaving school, he was able to plant these cuttings, and around some 2,000 dahlias, in the first year. So for the next nine months, with no real income and surviving on saved stock money, my father was rewarded with acres of flowers.

The dahlias were to be his pride and joy. They were not a cut flower that many market traders liked to sell in the 1950s, because they required more care and attention than most, but my father was able to grow them, cut them fresh and sell them from his stall, thus bypassing Covent Garden completely.

My father bought several new varieties of dahlia that had been propagated, and they were something new on the Surrey Street scene. A few other traders started selling them but my father grew dahlias of the most vibrant colours, and he attributed this to the fish manure which he used. He also used this on his tomatoes, and they had a wonderful flavour. He would leave them to ripen on the plant for the fullest flavour and the fish

A well-loved but somewhat damaged photograph of the author, with Bruno, the family dog, in the spring of the first year on the Woodcote smallholding -1958.

manure gave the tomatoes a slightly salty taste.

He was rewarded with queues of customers at his stall. My father's tomatoes were more expensive than those of other market traders, but customers, aplenty, bought from my father's stall for the simple fact that they knew his tomatoes really were homegrown.

It is unfortunate, nowadays, that they are picked green and then allowed to ripen en route to the shops. My father believes that only if the tomato is ripened on the plant is its true flavour developed.

By 1958, my father was growing flowers for all-year-round sales and he also continued with the plants into the bedding season.

He remembers when the bedding plants were once packed in kipper boxes, 18 roots to a box. These kipper boxes were sold to the nurserymen, because they were ideal containers for plants.

In the early years, certain plants were dug up, straight from the ground. A root ball would be made by squeezing the root and soil together, forming a spherical shape, and the roots were then placed upright in the boxes. These were left, undisturbed, until they were displayed, and then sold, on the stall.

Bedding plants were usually sold in quantities and they were dug out, perhaps a dozen at a time, by the fingers, and then the plants were wrapped in newspaper for the customer.

At the very end of a busy, bedding plant season,

Our smallholding at Woodcote, showing the 'chrysanthemum success ' - 1959.

David William Lovett jnr.: 'another good year' - 1960.

my father told me that his fingers would be blood raw from the grit in the compost,

My father grew well over half of his flowers and about a third of his own plants. The only flowers he did not grow were the spring selection of tulips, daffodils, iris and bulbs, as these were all bought in.

He continued working on the smallholding and stall and was to experience the very severe winter of 1963 - The 'Big Freeze.' There were to be Arctic conditions which began about the Christmas Eve of 1962.

Flowers froze in the containers, on the stall, and every bunch taken out of the tins had lumps of ice attached to it. It was weather that nobody relished, least of all my father.

Brenda, our helper, working on Bill's flower stall in 1961: all home-grown!

Being a florist and nurseryman was a precarious occupation, to say the least. The only solution was to sell everything on the stall at half-price and try to clear the day's stock.

This particular winter was to last almost three months, with blizzards, snow drifts and freezing night temperatures. Severe gales damaged most of my father's greenhouses.

With glass broken, attempting to heat the greenhouses was futile. All his stock was wiped out, not just a year's worth of growth but many years of work was destroyed.

My father carried on in a small way, working the land throughout 1963 and into 1964, but with stock money depleted, after the previous severe winter, he decided the stall, and smallholding, were too much to handle.

Bill taking a break at Little Woodcote smallholding, in 1961.

Bill Lovett at the stall in Surrey Street, c.1938. The kipper boxes contained root plants.

His love of plants and flowers encouraged him to continue, but he moved to a smaller plot. He has lived for many years on Telegraph Track, which is now included in the Sutton Countryside Walk, a leaflet issued by the Downlands Project and the London Borough of Sutton.

Although he is now retired he still enjoys growing plants and flowers, especially Bonsai trees, and he also enjoys painting.

He was commissioned by the Surrey Street Federation Association, to paint a picture of old-time Surrey Street, and this was presented to the Mayor, Pat Hecks, in July 1993, together with my father's hand-painted scroll which described the Surrey Street characters which are depicted in the picture on this page. Today the painting hangs in Croydon Town Hall.

Although my father was not able to pass down Walter's original stall to his offspring, as we were all too young at the time and later followed different careers, he gave us something more valuable, and that is a love and appreciation of plants and flowers.

This is not the end of the Lovett's Stall Story, however. It continues with Bert and Olive Lovett, on the second family stall 'up the top.'

Bill Lovett, left, with Croydon's Mayor, Pat Hecks, at a Town Hall reception in 1993, when Bill presented his painted scroll, to accompany the oil painting shown below.

Bill Lovett, in 1993, with his oil painting of old time Surrey Street. The scene shows Walter near his stall and George Thorogood against a wall on the right, holding his grand-daughter's hand.

Up the top

Firmly-established

Herbie Lovett's success - a complete show of all his produce. He is pictured close to his display, with Mr. Durrant, owner of the private market in the centre of Horsham and Jim Harding, right, who worked for Herbie in the early 1950s, when this picture was taken. Note the hoops on the Almeria grape barrels, which were used for stubbing up (see p.24).

It was in the 1930s that the Lovett family ran two stalls, side-by-side. The second stall had been licensed by my Uncle Herbie, one of the older brothers, who relinquished his stall just before the war, to go to Horsham.

In that town he became very successful, owning two shops in the heart of the town, running several stalls and selling wholesale.

Uncle Bert took on Uncle Herbie's stall in 1946, thereby ensuring our 100 years of trading. My father relinquished his stall in 1964, but from 1946 the two brothers worked side-by-side. Uncle Bert had returned from the Second World War, after being stationed in India and Burma for three years, with the East Surrey Regiment. Upon his return he did not take up his previous occupation, as a roofer and tiler, but decided to help the family business to survive. The elder brothers and sisters were married and following different careers, so it was left to the younger brothers, Bert and Bill, to take over.

So, together, the brothers worked the two stalls and slowly built up the business.

Bert preferred to work on the land in Mitcham, and buy produce from Covent Garden, as well as travelling around to local suppliers, buying stock. However, local suppliers could be many miles away, anywhere in the Thames Valley or the Home Counties. In those days there were no garden centres in the immediate vicinity, as there are now, and so these market gardens were regarded as 'local.' Bert continued working the land for many years, where he would toil all day, preparing the soil and planting out delphiniums, lupins and all the main herbaceous plants, wallflowers and vegetables such as cabbages, broccoli, sprouts, sweetcorn, tomatoes, marrow and even a few aubergines.

The land was approximately one-and-a-half acres in size and Uncle Bert would work well into the evenings, until eight or nine o'clock in the summer months. Even in the winter, weather and light permitting, Bert would be found working on the land as late as possible.

Then came the time when the two brothers worked independently, side-by-side though, but attending to their own stalls and buying their own stocks. They did not wish to be in competition with each other so each deviated, slightly, from Walter's stocks of plants. My father kept some of Walter's lines, including the rock plants and cheap bedding varieties, antirrhinums and stocks. These he sold in large quantities, very cheaply and on a daily basis when they were in season.

Bert kept to the larger pots, including spring bulbs and flowers, fruit trees, rose bushes, climbers such as honeysuckle and clematis, as well as continuing along the same lines as Walter for plants such as hydrangea, rhododendrons and large geraniums, which were still being supplied to the middle and upper classes, with the larger gardens, which were still in evidence in the 1950s.

One of Bert's suppliers for the larger variety of plants was Milton Hutchings, a family-run nursery, which supplied the Royal Family, were involved in floral displays, Royal shows and exhibitions, and who had large nurseries selling wholesale at Covent Garden.Walter bought from the supplier's own nurseries before the Second World War and Uncle Bert continued trading with them.

Bert, Agnes and Bill Lovett pictured in Surrey Street in 1951.

This picture, taken during the 1940s, includes Bert Lovett and Lal, the paper gal, who delivered newspapers to some of the stallholders and carried out odd jobs for Winnie Conners.

During the '1960S AND 1970S a comfortable living was realized from the stall. The market place was thriving and the plantsmen and fruit and veg. traders alike, had plenty of customers. People wouldn't just saunter down Surrey Street, but go to the market place and buy in quantity. It made sense for the market trader to buy in bulk, because he or she had the trade in those days. Bert had no competition from garden centres, they had not become the fashion, then, and only a few market gardens existed for the general public, so Uncle Bert's business flourished.

My uncle also bought direct from the Dutch growers. Stolwyk and Turnhout were big importers and he bought direct from these suppliers in the 1960s and 1970s. They would deliver to Church Path yard, using large vans called pantechnicons, delivering as many as 100 baskets. These were circular, approximately five feet in height, containing all their bulbs, crocuses, hyacinths and both climber and bush roses as well as perennial plants which would be stocked and stacked, seven-feet high, and would take up most of the yard. The importer's invoices could sometimes total as much as £1,000. Bert would pay by cheque, by return. Instalments were out of the question. This was an incredible amount of money to pay for one order, even in the '60s.

It is very difficult for the younger person to appreciate, today, the money aspect. In the earlier years one could obtain a lot of produce for one's money, but today's prices make a mockery of yesteryear. Then, a little money went a long way - that is not so today.

The 1970s and 1980s saw Bert still buying in bulk, buying direct from the importers and bypassing Covent Garden, but the mid-'80s brought about a gradual decline in the trade, with more and more garden centres opening, supermarkets selling plants and cut flowers, and car boot sales having stallholders doing the same.

I suppose it's true, to a certain extent, that competition makes for trade, but fierce competition, during the 1980s and 1990s, has been killing trade for the small businessman.

Over the decades, Bert and Olive's stall moved 'south,' in position. When a stall became vacant they moved up a place and finally ended 'up the top,' which is where they are today. The three

Olive and Bert Lovett, left and right, with Jackie Prattley, helper, in 1994.

Up the top end (south end) of Surrey Street in the 1980s.

words, 'up the top,' were those adopted by the family when answering the whereabouts of another member of the family. "Just going up the top," was a familiar expression.

Although Bert and Olive are now officially retired, Uncle Bert still works very much behind the scenes, whilst Olive still stands and serves at the stall, in pouring rain, brilliant sunshine, bitter cold or blustery winds, just as she has been doing for the past 45 years, taking time off only very occasionally.

Bert prefers to buy the produce and help his son, Ian, who now runs the stall with his wife, Rosanna, 'packing out' and 'packing up' the stall.

Ian and Bert visit local nurseries, and other suppliers, which takes up most of the week in the busy season, and they are rewarded with good quality and variety on the stall - all year round shows of colour which they display to the customers with great splendour.

When the bedding plant season is in full swing, and I view their customers and stall from a distance, I am reminded of bees round a honey pot, tasting the sweet delights of summer!

Early 1980s to present day

Rose's garden

My cousins, Ian Lovett and his wife, Rosanna, are the current stallholders "up the top" in Surrey Street. When his parents retired, some ten years ago, because of Uncle Bert's ill-health, Ian decided to leave his employer, British Telecom.

This was no new ground for Ian, who had accompanied Bert around local suppliers and growers, taken trips to Covent Garden, and helped him on the land in Mitcham. His first taste of salesmanship started at an early age when he set up two orange boxes under the archway in Church Path, selling Bert's 'leftovers' and unwanted plants, to passers-by who walked through into North End.

Like Uncle Jack, Ian and Rosanna have other talents and until 1992 were also working in a semi - professional capacity in the entertainment business, in the shape of a band, called Rainbow's End. Rosanna, a singer, appeared with Ian, the drummer, at venues in London and elsewhere. They had contracts with Mecca and played at large venues, cocktail functions, firms' dinner dances and other functions.

One of their local residencies was the Selsdon Park Hotel, near Croydon, but market trading has taken up most of their time in recent years, so entertainment has taken a back seat.

Customers have affectionately dubbed the stall "Rose's garden." The presentation of plants reveals an interesting and varied selection, something that has taken precedence throughout the Lovetts' trading. The slogan on their sign reads: "Whatever the season, there is always something for the garden." Rosanna and Ian take immense pride in their stocks of plants and flowers, and their extensive knowledge is passed on to their customers. They cater to clients' requirements, whether it be gardening advice, making hanging baskets to order, Christmas table arrangements, floral displays for public houses and hotel foyers, weddings or funerals.

They sell a much wider range of plants and flowers today. Shrubs are not so highly sought after, of late. Herbaceous plants are the trend, along with plants for water gardens and Meditteranean gardens, with customers wanting exotic plants, and the cottage garden look has returned, whether the buyer lives in a small town house or country house, the demand is the same. Customers want plants that require no aftercare. The fashion for conservatories, which are double-glazed and heated, means that more varieties of plants can be sought from growers. In demand

Ian and Rosanna Lovett, the current stallholders, at their plant stall in 1993.

are palms, ferns and Bougainvilleas, for example, which thrive in such conditions. Japanese gardening is another fad and the atmosphere of ferns, bonsais and acers has become very fashionable.

Fruit plants have always been popular and are still a good mainstay, but today's customers require containerized plants, such as cordon type apple and plum trees. The ballerina-type fruit plants are also popular but traditional vegetables are still in great demand.

Plants, be they exotic or unusual, are no longer a 'class' commodity as they were in Walter's day. Now they are affordable by almost everyone. Television gardening programmes and magazines have opened up a whole new perspective and people now have the confidence to say what they want, rather than ask what is for sale.

Time and space for plants are the customers' considerations these days and so, too, for a market trader. That is why Ian and Rosanna, being more adventurous than most, decided to exhibit at the Hampton Court Flower Show in 1992, displaying anything from the exotic to the topiary. Housed in their own marquee, exhibiting every day for one week, they put on for show and sale 'lollipop' bay trees, lavateras and ceanothus, arranged on large sticks, large, potted ornate conifers and unusual hanging basket arrangements, which could not normally be shown in the market place.

Ian and Rosanna won a contract in 1993 to design, plan and supply plants for a company hiring a reception room at the Savoy Hotel in London, and worked on plant colour schemes to match the room.

The contract lasted for a year, during which they carried out similar work at various hotels and for the National Exhibition Centre, Birmingham.

They have had numerous offers to do landscaping, but lack of time means they have had to decline. They hope their sons, Chris and Gary, who already show some interest in the trade,

Rosanna Lovett at her flower stall in November 1994.

The Royal visit in November 1994, viewed through the Lovett plant stall. HRH Prince Charles is talking to Jackie Prattley; on her right is John Williams, Surrey Street Federation chairman.

might go into this side of the business later, but Rosanna had gone into landscaping in a miniaturized fashion in Surrey Street. When customers are dubious about matching plant colours or heights, Rosanna will demonstrate with the plants, arranging them on the footpath and up on the steps, to give the customers ideas.

In 1994 they decided to expand their business further and Rosanna took on a stall virtually opposite their plant stall but selling cut flowers. This was once part of the Lovett trade - Walter, Uncle Bert and my father all grew most of their own cut flowers and Ian and Rosanna felt it was time to diversify. Again, competition at close quarters, competition from garden centres, supermarkets and even car boot fairs, are a threat to the business. However, lack of trade on the plant stall in the slack season means some revenue is ensured from the flower stall.

Car boot fairs cause Ian wasted time and inconvenience, inasmuch as the boot fair trader consumes the market, buying from the suppliers and growers in fairly large quantities, making it difficult for the market traders to purchase his stocks. It seems incredible, but demand is now outstripping supply. Ideally, Ian would like to run his own garden centre, where he and Rosanna could display a much wider variety, but the market place is still an attractive proposition as a small business. With its low overheads they can undercut the garden centres and the passing trade benefits from these lower prices.

A new trend, brought about in the early 1990s by the car boot fairs it is believed, is 'bartering.'

Some customers will actually 'haggle' for plants and shrubs. Ian and Rosanna find this rather distasteful. They are made offers for plants or asked to sell two plants for the price of one. The market place is already a location where one can buy cheaply. It is an old-fashioned market, even today, and they feel that this new fad should be discontinued, to let the market retain its dignity.

Ian and Rosanna also feel very strongly about Surrey Street and that it should receive investment. They hope that it will become a co-operative in the forseeable future, but with each stall an individual concern, the stallholders united, controlling their own market and vetting new traders, as well as, perhaps, giving the market a continental flavour, with a cobbled street and continental awnings.

In the course of an interview by the *Croydon Advertiser* in 1993, Rosanna said: "I think there's still a trade for markets. But I don't know if it will be for another 100 years. It's nice to keep it in the family."

I, too, hope that one or both of their sons will continue the family tradition. Only time will tell.

Pre-war and post-war

The toy stall

To be or not to be... a market trader

Captain Wombell, lion trainer, of the Bostock and Wombells circus. Jack, right, aged 16 years, who was just starting out in show business, won a bet of £50, for standing in the lion's den for five minutes. He needed the money to help to pay for a badly-needed hip operation, for his sister, in 1923.

Market traders come from all walks of life. Many have talents besides being stallholders and my Uncle Jack (Garcia) was no exception. Jack, of Jewish descent, was born in 1907. He was to have quite a chequered career before settling down to market trading in Surrey Street.

At the age of 14, Jack left home in Camberwell, London. He worked in theatre and, later with the great comedian, Will Hay, toured Australia, New Zealand and South Africa where, in the latter country, Jack performed in a Royal Command Performance for the Prince of Wales, who later became the King who abdicated - the Duke of Windsor. As well as touring abroad, Jack also travelled around Great Britain with the famous 'Will Hay Sketches.' These sketches ran for some 15 years and Jack appeared in them as one of the 'cheeky schoolboys,' whilst Will Hay played the part of a schoolmaster, complete with cane and

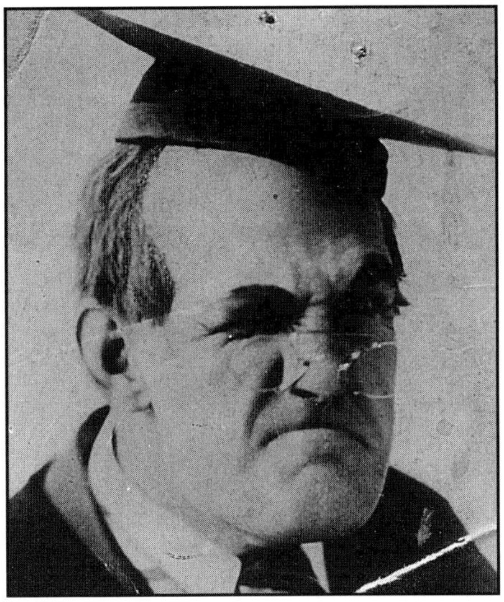

Will Hay snr, in the late 1920s.

Jack and Betty's show business calling card in the 1930s.

mortarboard.

Whilst on tour Jack met my Aunt Betty, in a show called 'Out of Work.' She was a 'pony girl' (pony is the name for dancers under five feet tall and 'tillers' is the term used for the taller, 'high kickers'). They decided to team up together and create their own double act, so Jack left the Will

Betty Lovett - a stage photograph c.1920.

Hay sketches.

Their new act consisted of Uncle Jack playing the ukulele whilst Betty sang and danced. She performed ballet, tap and acrobatics and, also being a contortionist, she could shape herself like a paperclip and leave the audience aghast at her physical feats.

They performed on tour together throughout Britain and their act was used to fill in 'gaps' while new sets were put on stage, or they would be classed as 'number four' performers of a show perhaps with the Crazy Gang or Max Miller being the number one spots, especially at the home of the Crazy Gang - the Victoria Theatre, in London. Here they worked alongside all the big stars of their day such as Nellie Wallis, Arthur Prince, Charlie Coneys, Renee Houston and many others.

Jack and Betty's 10-minute double act would go something like this: Jack would play the ukulele and Betty would sing and dance, then Jack would tell a joke or recite a poem or a dramatic monologue, such as this one called *Suicide?*

He sits alone in a darkened room
Alone in the fading light
Why is his brow so heavy with bloom
And his cheeks so deadly white?
But though his heart is sick with care
His courage never blenches,
His eyes are fixed in a glassy stare
What is it? His firm hand clenches
A little courage, he murmurs, yes,
A little and all is won

A croaking gurgle more or less
A gasp, the deed is done
Without a shudder or eyelid wink
It makes the heart recoil,
That he so truly calmly drank
A dose of CASTOR OIL....

Betty on stage in the late 1920s.

Jack needed to find regular employment once he and Betty married, so theatre life ceased for a few years whilst he worked as a telephone engineer in Kensington. He transferred to Croydon where Agnes found them accommodation - the house next door to her and Walter, in Church Path. Betty had two children, Miriam, in 1931 and Leon, born in 1938.

Leon was to become quite successful in show business in the 1950s and 1960s, working in live radio shows, television plays and films, and he also appeared in the long-running stage show South Pacific with Mary Martin and Wilbur Evans, at the Theatre Royal in Drury Lane, London. Leon played the part of Jerome.

It was about the early 1930s that Uncle Jack managed to take part in a wild west show in Kennards 'arcade' in Croydon. The show ran for around six to eight weeks and had a variety of performers, including Hawaiian dancers and real-life Canadian Indians called Chief Blue Sky, Little Calf and his wife, Princess Mora.

They appeared performing acrobatics whilst riding horses bareback. Uncle Jack dressed as a Zorro-type character, all in black with a white, patterned, Mexican-style shirt, he also rode horseback.

Jack Garcia, looking the part in the 1930s.

Jack was then out of work. His father's relatives had been in market trading for the past 200 years, their haunts being Petticoat Lane and East Lane markets in London, so it wasn't surprising to find Jack working in Surrey Street. He started out by selling 'swag.' The definition of swag is 'stolen goods,' but Jack's were definitely 'kosher!' He sold razor blades, chocolates, powder puff boxes with handkerchiefs, sewn on by Betty and Miriam, which they sold for 6d. ($2\frac{1}{2}$p), for two boxes.

Leon Garcia, relaxing off stage in the mid-1950s.

Whilst Jack was employed in Surrey Street, Will Hay paid him a visit at Church Path, and asked him if he would return to the stage and teach Will Hay jnr. the 'schoolmaster' sketches and start him

Jack Garcia as a 'Zorro'-type Western cowboy in the mid-1930s.

Chief Blue Sky, appearing with The Last of the Mohicans in the mid-1930s.

Betty and Jack Garcia on their 'swag' stall in Surrey Street, during the early 1950s.

off in the theatre. This was about 1936. Jack, and Charlie Harvey, who had worked with Jack on a regular basis, agreed, and taught Will Hay jnr. all they knew, touring with him, and performing the sketches, all over England.

The Second World War interrupted any further theatricals, on the home front, for Jack. He joined the R.A.F. and was involved with entertainment for ENSA (the Entertainment National Service Association).

After the war, demobbed and back home, Jack found employment prospects grim so he returned to Surrey Street. Jack's acting career continued, though. His stall was his stage, his customers were his audience and Surrey Street was his theatre, where he would give 'live performances' to the crowds who passed through.

Jack bought and sold bankrupt stock, insurance fire-damaged stock, dresses, slippers, groceries and other lines. Eventually he was renting a shop in Church Street, running two stalls, plus a shop in Dorking, Surrey, which Miriam managed. All these outlets meant that Jack could buy and sell, in bulk.

Above: Jack Garcia, as the cheeky schoolboy, Will Hay jnr. and Charlie Harvey as Jimmy Arbuckle, in the Schoolmaster's sketch, during the mid-1930s. Right: Jack Garcia, beside an ENSA concert poster, in Calais in 1946.

Christmas fairies in Surrey Street

Toy time 1960s-1980s

Betty Garcia (1905 - 1963), on the toy stall with the fairy dolls which "an old lady made." This photograph was taken in the 1950s.

In the early 1960s Jack changed his pitch from outside Milletts, and took over a stall closer to the middle of Surrey Street, but still selling 'swag' and toys, too, at Christmas time. Jack bought clowns' heads, Betty and Miriam made the clowns' bodies and they also made hand puppets which they sold for 6d. (2½p) each.

The family bought large quantities of cellophane bags and filled them with painting books, crayons, whistles, bracelets, rings and watches, similar to a Christmas stocking today, and sold them at 2/6d (12½p) per bag. They made, and sold, these by the gross, in the late 1940s and early 1950s.

The atmosphere by the toy stall would sometimes be quite electric when Jack, Betty and Miriam were giving 'live' performances, to draw the crowd and entice them to buy. Jack's patter would go something like this: "Now, what have I got here? I've got these razor blades. You buy them two bob a packet in the shops. I don't want two bob a packet. I don't even want a shilling a packet. I'll give you something special. I'll give you three packets for sixpence, who wants them?"

Miriam and Betty would then point their forefingers in different directions towards the crowd (which by now had oozed sideways, blocking Leg Lemon's stall and the stall on the other side of Jack's, much to their annoyance, I'm sure), and

Betty and Miriam would say, alternately: "Yes, and sold to that lady over there," and: "over here, yes sir, three packets you want? Sold, thank you, sir."

Those people in the 'audience' would then look at their 'neighbours,' or behind them, to see who was buying and were always convinced that they were genuine customers, and would then open their purses and wallets and readily think Jack was selling a bargain.

Compared with shop prices, he was. That is the attraction of a market.

My Aunt Betty made the fairy doll outfits but the customers were told that they were made by an old lady who was crippled with rheumatoid arthritis. Sadly it was to be this complaint which was the main cause of her early death in 1963, at the age of 58 years.

Miriam would dress other dolls in Elizabethan costume, which were also sold for the Christmas trade. This was the time of rationing. They were only allocated two dozen dolls which they easily sold in two days of trading.

The Christmas scene down Surrey Street, in years gone by, was something rather special. I remember the sight being very picturesque with most traders making an effort to decorate their stalls. Stalls were allowed to be packed out all night, especially the night before Christmas Eve.

Each 'family' took turns in guarding their stalls, whilst other traders returned with further supplies or went home for a few hours' sleep. Our stall contained several forms of decoration, all saleable goods of course, such as the Christmas trees, sprigs of mistletoe, crosses and wreaths.

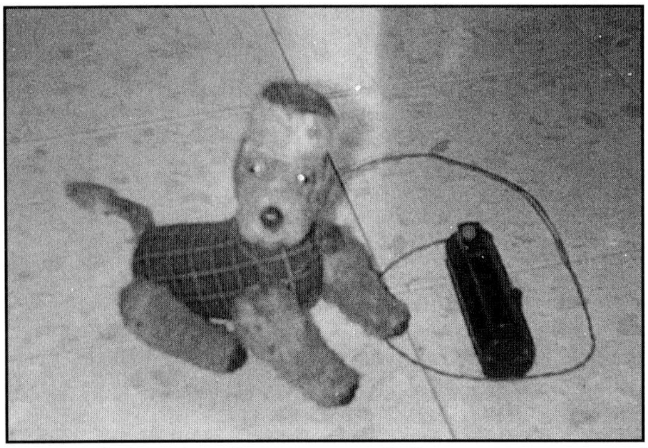

One of the tin, fur-covered, battery-operated toys; it walked to the count of ten, stopped and sat, then barked four times before it stood up and walked on. These toys were seen c. 1960.

A Christmas scene, in Surrey Street, in the 1990s.

The toy stall would be decorated with Christmas tree lights, tinsel, glitter and numerous fairy dolls, all, again, for sale.

The toys which Betty and Jack sold on their stall in the 1950s and 1960s were quite comical and would have had great difficulty, today, in passing the safety regulations.

The Black Russian bears were battery-operated toys. The bear held a drinking glass, clasped in one paw, and a cola drink bottle in the other. Once liquid was poured into his glass, and the battery was running, the bear's eyes would light up and he'd drink from the glass.

The liquid appeared to go down his throat but, in fact, went down a tube in his arm, across to the other arm, then back into the cola bottle, whereupon the bear would then pour out another glass of liquid.

They sold pigs (Pinky and Perky), that squeaked and swayed from side to side whilst tossing two 'fried eggs' from a frying pan. The toy was 'timed' so that the pan was positioned to catch the fried eggs, which inverted on their descent and landed as a 'rasher of bacon.'

Monkeys smoking cigarettes were another toy. These, again, were battery-operated and, once switched on, could be given a real cigarette, already lit, which the monkey would then inhale. The smoke would come out of its nostrils, in the form of smoke rings.

A fire chief's car, battery-operated, would move along, ringing its bell, and with the telephone ringing inside its cab. The fireman next to the driver would lift the receiver and 'talk,' his head going up and down.

When he talked the car remained stationary, but once he replaced the receiver the car would continue moving again with its bell clanging.

Sadly the curtains closed for my Uncle Jack, and he died in December 1994, at the age of 87 years. I was fortunate to be able to see him in Israel, shortly before he passed away, and was able to record his stories with the help of his daughter, Miriam.

He was one of the 'real' characters down Surrey Street, in his day, and will long be remembered.

Jack Garcia (1907 - 1994), retired from Surrey Street when he was 80 years old. This photograph, taken not long before his death, shows Jack in Israel, where he went to live with his daughter, Miriam, in 1993.

King of the oranges

Old-established market traders

Jaffa Joe, the 'slack' buyer

Although my father, and his brother, Herbie, gave Joe the nickname 'The Outspan King,' on account of his purchases of Outspan oranges which were imported from South Africa, he is better remembered as Jaffa Joe. Jaffa oranges were always being shipped over from Palestine (now Israel), and these became his main 'draw line.'

Joe Jarman rented a stall outside the old jailhouse, in Surrey Street, opposite to Walter's stall, and used to store his produce in the disused jail. His trips to Covent Garden to Pouparts, in Long Acre, were to buy all the 'slack' oranges - those in damaged packages. Joe would buy boxes that had been damaged en route or boxes which were short in their contents.

These could not be sold in the usual manner because, in those days, oranges were sold at a standard number per crate. Any with shortages would therefore be classed as 'slack.'

Joe would sometimes buy by the lorry load, more often the boatload, purchasing slack right

The old Jail House, Surrey Street, photographed around 1937.

'Jaffa Joe,' Joe Jarman (1890 - 1961).

through the boat, going direct to the docks to collect his goods and bring them back to the jail-house for storage and sale.

He was a good customer at Pouparts and had the monopoly of all the slack there. No-one else got a look in, as far as my father, and the other traders, knew.

He 'guaranteed' his slack, not by backhanders but by handing a signed, blank cheque over the counter.

Once he had bought his slack the amount spent would be written in and then he would guarantee his next order by handing over another signed, blank cheque. Pouparts knew that Joe would buy all the slack they had. No matter how the trade was, Joe never refused to buy.

When Joe died, a lorry full of wreaths was sent along, together with another from the porters at Covent Garden.

The family still exists today, in Surrey Street. In recent times one of the younger sons has continued the business farther down the street.

Costermonger barrows in the streets

The fruit merchant

Bill Curd's family is another old-established trading family of Surrey Street and was there before licences were issued.

Bill's parents owned a yard and stable in Grace Road, West Croydon, both of which were essential when trading in the market place because very few storage facilities were available in Surrey Street itself in those days.

As well as running several stalls in Surrey Street, Bill Curd's parents were also hawkers and traded between North End and West Croydon station, using the original costermonger barrows. At the turn of this century, London's costermongers and street hawkers numbered around 60,000. Costermongers were originally apple sellers and the name is derived from the costard, a native apple, which was very large and sour and well-known in the eighteenth century.

The hawkers' hand barrows had to be on the move all the time, unless they were actually trading, and even then they could only stop for a short period before having to move on. This type of trading continued until about the mid-1920s, when traffic increased in volume and made it almost impossible for this type of trade to be continued along the high street, because the barrows were a nuisance.

The police would confiscate goods, and barrows, after warnings had been given, so that marked the end of the North End hand-barrow trading. Pedlars' Paradise then ceased to exist.

Between the First and Second World Wars, Bill Curd's father had a flourishing wholesale fruit business and three retail greengrocery shops. He became the biggest dealer in horses and ponies in the South of England, during the Second World War, taking advantage of the petrol shortage. He bought both harness and saddle horses from Wales, around 1,000 each year, which were transported by rail and sold on to tradespeople such as the United Dairies milk firm, bakers and greengrocers.

Bill Curd's father also sold horses to the army, which were used by the mounted Home Guard in

Bill Curd, snr. (1894-1977) pictured in 1975.

East Anglia.

Bill Curd apparently operated in a different way to my father and other traders. He never went to Covent Garden for his produce, but to Spitalfields and Borough Market, where there were auctions. He would view samples of fruit from the various 'lots,' before the auction.

Two or three sample boxes would be sent to the auctioneer's room and the buyers would judge the quality of the fruit, perhaps viewing one or two hundred samples, before buying. They would also judge the standard of deterioration. In the early years, fruit began to rot much more quickly, because there was no refrigeration. Bill Curd would attend these auctions, along with

Surrey Street market traders, in their own street, after bringing produce from Borough Market in 1910.

commissioning agents representing fruit shops all over England, and each agent would be commissioned to buy perhaps as many as 100 boxes of fruit for their customers.

Imported fruit came mainly to the London docks but would sometimes be taken as far as Southampton, Cardiff, Hull, Liverpool and the South Coast docks. The fruit cargo was generally brought up the Thames Estuary on boats. This is now a thing of the past. Docks have closed and the Thames is no longer used for the importation of produce, most of which is now carried in lorries from the continent. The next job was to collect the goods from the docks. This was a time-consuming task because everything was man-handled then, with no modern machinery to speed up the process. The produce was contained in heavy, cumbersome packages. Full barrels contained 10-12 dozen pounds of apples. There were also half barrels, 22lb. weight barrels and bushels holding 36-40lbs. Half-bushel baskets held cherries or plums, perhaps, and these weighed 18-20lbs. Then there were pecks, little round baskets holding 12-14lbs, as well as wooden and wicker rounds and also barrels. It was a nightmare, loading them on to a lorry, but for Bill Curd and my grandfather, Walter, this task was eased slightly because they owned lorries which were like the old trolleys which used to be horse-drawn. The design was such that the sides of the vehicle, which were called 'raves,' would actually guide the round load in towards the centre of the lorry. There were rarely any tumbles.

Packing the goods was a laborious task but another problem presented itself at the docks. London dockers were notorious for striking. Arguments with the Port of London Authority frequently broke out over low pay or shortage of men for a particular job, or over bad weather, so they could not expect to collect their goods from more than one dock in a day, unless the docks were close together.

Bill Curd operated in this way and bypassed Covent Garden. He would have received his goods perhaps one day ahead of the London wholesale markets and would come directly back to Surrey Street with his produce to 'set them alight,' meaning he would have a buyer's market. In addition to being a fruit merchant, Bill Curd was also the first chairman of the Surrey Street Federation, back in the 1950s. The association still exists today and operates in a fashion similar to a union, looking after the interests of the market traders and its 'birthplace.' In the earlier years there was a waiting list of approximately 200 people who were waiting for stalls. Interviewing, which still takes place, determined whether a would-be trader had sufficient stock money, transport and other necessities. The association preferred family members taking on stalls. That was one of its aims, as old-established families wanted their offspring to continue and would even help the market traders with loans.

The association was also involved with many charities, supporting the nearby Ellis Davis Homes for the Elderly, with each family receiving fruit, vegetable and grocery hampers in addition to winter coal, each Christmas. St. Christopher's School for handicapped children, in Croydon, was presented with toys, fruit, sweets, and a Christmas party each year. In the summer, the pupils were treated to seaside outings. The association also gave generously to other appeals.

Bill Curd retired to live in Eastbourne, Sussex, but his family still carries on the business in Surrey Street.

On a barrow, from Wandsworth to Croydon

The Harts

The Harts are another very long-established trading family of Surrey Street. Mark Hart's grandfather used to walk with his barrow from Wandsworth to Surrey Street, daily. Needless to say, when a house, along with yard and stabling, became available in Hancroft Road, Croydon, his grandfather and family took up occupancy.

Mark's grandfather was another trader who 'ran' for his pitch before the licences were issued. This entailed the trader choosing his pitch, putting a wooden baton down across the site selected, standing back two or three yards in a shop doorway, or back on to the pavement, and waiting for the policeman to blow his whistle. Then the market trader would go and collect his trestle, or stall, and put it in the place which had been reserved. It was unusual for anyone to move the baton, once it had been put in place, but occasionally fights would break out when batons were moved. This particular method was not unique to Surrey Street and other markets and fairgrounds operated in the same way. Poles were placed on selected pitches when traders arrived at a new venue. They would then stand and wait at their allotted places, sometimes for many hours until the whistle blew, just to make

Leonard (Tiny) Hart (1867-1960) founder of the Hart business, outside his stables in Hancroft Road, Croydon, soon after the Second World War ended.

The Harts' stall in the 1940s, with customers queueing for vegetables.

Radio and television journalist, Richard Dimbleby, left, interviewing Mark Hart, right, when the BBC visited The Roundel Club, Croydon, in June 1947.

sure of the best position possible.

At one time the Hart family had three stalls, supplying fruit and vegetables, in Surrey Street, very close to the Dog and Bull public house. The source of supply was the Borough Market, which claims to be London's oldest fruit and vegetable market and which dates back to mediaeval times. It deals with small distributors, such as grocers and market traders and most of the Harts' stock came from this market. Their main line was cauliflowers. From the customers' point of view, this may have seemed an easy living, but a view from behind the scenes revealed a stallholder waist-high in wet cauliflower leaves and stalks which were cut off prior to display. Mark, and his brother, wore the porters' working aprons which were made of leather and able to withstand the sharp razor cuts which the knives made as the thick, outer leaves, were being removed. Both men were to finish up with arthritis because of the permanent wet patches on their shoulders, produced by humping wet, hessian sacks on to the top of the sheds in the Dog and Bull Yard.

Mark was interviewed, in his capacity as a boxer, by the radio and television personality, Richard Dimbleby.

The interview, which took place in June 1947 and was for the radio programme called *Down Your Way,* took place in the yard at the back of the Dog and Bull pub.

After the initial interview, and while Mark was still being recorded, he was asked his choice of music for the programme. He chose *Let bygones be Bygones*, much to his fianceé's displeasure! Mark and his wife were to enjoy their retirement years at Banstead, Surrey. One of their family was to continue to operate a stall, selling cauliflowers, in Surrey Street.

Beetroot cooked in a big old copper pot

'Big firm' (The Toohig family)

The Toohig family originated from County Clare, on the west coast of Ireland, but were living in England before the turn of this century. They were another old-established trading family who had stalls in Surrey Street before licences were granted and they were to become extremely successful in market trading.

There were two brothers, Patsy and Jim, who were both involved in running stalls in Surrey Street. Jim usually went 'on the rounds' with his horse and cart and it was Patsy who became known as "The Big Firm," having many concerns in, and out, of Surrey Street. He never worked on the stalls in Surrey Street but employed other men to run them because he was involved in all the buying from Covent Garden and Spitalfields, making him more like a wholesaler. His line was mainly fruit, which he would obtain from various orchards in Kent.

In common with many of the original stallholders, local accommodation for stabling and a yard, were vital to house all the produce, horse, cart and stalls. The Toohig's yard and stables were in Devonshire Road, Croydon, where they would stock anything from Christmas trees to wild ponies.

Jim's stall supplied a variety of salads. The family cooked their own beetroot, hundredweights of it, in a big, old, copper pot, and when the business was at its height they would cook beetroot all day long in their Devonshire Road yard. That is still one of the most messy jobs to undertake today. Another, many decades ago, must also have been celery. It was the filthiest of the salad items with which to deal, because of the way in which it was grown. Today it is grown 'clean,' being covered with black polythene bags whilst in growth, and special varieties are cultivated which are 'self-blanching,' but years ago the market gardeners kept an area clear for the dirty process of celery-growing.

Celery has to be grown completely in the dark and this was once done, quite successfully, by using soot. Soot used to be given away, or sold, by the chimney sweeps to those people who had market gardens and allotments. The nurserymen would 'stand' the soot out in heaps for about a year, to be weathered. If this was not done then

Jim Toohig, snr. (1885 -1968) outside the old Croydon Printing Works in Surrey Street, c.1950s.

the harmful, acidic properties of the soot would have destroyed the celery. It also had another useful purpose - as a slug deterrent - and allotment holders used plenty of it.

The celery would be planted and covered by soil and soot combined. As the celery grew, the soot would be heaped higher, so as not to allow any light to reach it. Once fully grown, the celery would be pulled out pure white (today, it is more of a greeny-white). After buying the celery the market trader would have to wash each individual piece, using a galvanised bath full of cold water and a scrubbing brush. This had to be done to clean the soot from the outside of the celery before it could be displayed for sale on the stalls. This filthy operation left the operator smothered in black soot and, in the winter months, with chilblains on the hands, too.

Patsy was nicknamed 'The Controller,' because of the many concerns he established and controlled. He had connections in the New Forest for the trees and ponies which he dealt in. The Christmas trees would be bought in bulk and taken to Covent Garden and Spitalfields and sold wholesale. Around August each year he would go

to the Kent orchards and, with great expertise, judge the yields from each orchard and attend

Patsy Toohig (1892-1950), pictured in the New Forest c.1948.

local auctions to put in his bids. These orchards averaged anything from two to four acres in size. Patsy was very successful at this particular trade - good at estimating an accurate yield and knowing its worth.

Once the orchard harvest was bought, Patsy and his men would go to the orchards and pick the fruit, chiefly apples. The men would stay close to the crops, living in local accommodation or sleeping in tents or huts. Sometimes local people would be employed if extra manpower was needed. The men would return to trade on the stalls in Surrey Street during the week, because the fruit-picking was mainly carried out at weekends.

The ponies were another line and were bought in the New Forest, in Hampshire. These would be purchased, one or two at a time, and brought back to the Devonshire Road stables. Jim's sons, Jim, Bill and John, would break in these wild ponies around the perimeter of Croydon Cemetery, the area being green and free from the housing and traffic of today. It would take about a fortnight breaking in the ponies before they could be hired out to the local bakers and milkmen for use on their rounds.

Patsy was definitely an entrepreneur and, like my grandfather, Walter, was a very forward-thinking man. He thought, and built, big, to be successful. This he did with the installation of his banana - ripening room which he had built in his Devonshire Road premises along with cold storage facilities. He was probably the first local person to have a banana-ripening room and needed this for the large quantities of bananas he bought. This accommodation was to save time and money travelling to London wholesalers and to economize on wastage, too. He sold wholesale to local shops, greengrocers and to the Surrey Street market traders. Covent Garden had its own massive banana-ripening room so it was quite adventurous for an individual to do this, back in the 1930s.

The bananas were conveyed in their own special carriages, from abroad, and were contained in these until they reached their destination. Before the Second World War they came from the Canaries and would have arrived at Tilbury or the East India Docks, in London. They would then be put on the railway to King's Cross, or even East Croydon station, where there were ripening rooms opposite. The trade name in those days was Fyffe and this name applied to all bananas of quality. They arrived very dark green in colour and still on their stalks.

Once collected they would be taken to

Devonshire Road and housed in the specially-built ripening room. It had very low ceilings which were strong enough to take the tremendous weight of the bananas. Giant meat hooks were placed uniformly in the ceilings from which the bananas could hang. Bunches were then ripened to order by gas central heating supplied by pipes around the lower part of the walls.

The walk-in cold storage area was installed for pure convenience in the days of 'seasonal' produce.

Preserving edible produce, that had lengthy travelling time ahead, had to be catered for. The Canadian winesaps (apples), for example, used to be packed three bushels in a barrel, and the packers would interweave oily strips of tissue paper throughout the apples in the barrel, to keep them shiny but, more importantly, to stop them from drying out.

When cold storage was first introduced, and experimented with, a lot of mistakes were made, by selecting incorrect temperature settings, and both money and time were lost initially. John Toohig snr. remembered hundreds of boxes of Bramley cooking apples being spoilt and having to be thrown away. They came out of their cold storage very green, as they should look, but once cut open they were found to have turned very brown in colour. The cold storage was in its infancy around the 1930s, and this was another adventurous concern that became a successful operation for Patsy.

Patsy Toohig was also a valuable asset to the other market traders, in Surrey Street, before the Second World War. He provided transport for the other stallholders who could not afford to buy vehicles for collecting produce, so they relied on Patsy very much. This was another concern which earned him financial reward.

There was a lot of poverty around in those days and quite a number of traders from Surrey Street had insufficient funds to buy transport, or even their produce in bulk. These stallholders lived from day to day, to earn just a few shillings. When Patsy died, in 1950, the traders who had depended upon him for transport, had to go to the London wholesale markets themselves, by train, and then beg and borrow transport for the return journey. Some traders managed to obtain transport on a regular basis but for others it was a very hit-and-miss affair so cartage was organized and a lorry then operated from Surrey Street, to the London markets, to assist many of the traders to remain in business.

Patsy, like Walter and a few other traders, ran successful businesses. They were in the right place at the right time, with no competition to hinder them. The Toohig (pronounced 'twig') family have branches here and there and are still to be found in Surrey Street today, still surviving in the market place, together with a few other old, trading families.

A long view of the Surrey Street market in 1930.

'Son' and 'dad' were not related

Legs Lemon and Tiddler Knowles

Although neither was related, Tiddler Knowles called Hew 'Legs' Lemon "son" and the latter, in return called him "dad." They had worked together for many years and were always seen together. Legs was only 19 years old when he first started working for Tiddler, who was then in his mid-'50s, and was described as a "little dapper man, who was never seen without funds and who was fair and generous." He had a yard down Pitlake Bridge, behind the Coach and Horses public house, and this was where he kept all his root plants, apples and other items.

He was a big apple buyer, and used to go direct to the countryside, in Kent, attending and buying from auctions at Yalding, or sometimes buying direct from the farmers. His skill at judging the yield of an apple orchard equalled that of Patsy Toohig, and he, too, was to do this with great success, viewing orchards as large as four or five acres.

Like Walter, Tiddler was also a 'root man.' The pair of them also used to visit a local grower in Mitcham, known as "Barber's," buying pansies, Sweet Williams, Canterbury Bells and other varieties of plants. They bought their stock in bulk and sold in Surrey Street, on their own stalls, but keeping the price the same, so as not to undercut one another, even though they were at opposite ends of the market place so, even in those days, it seems the costermonger's law still existed.

Compared with today, the fruit season was of short duration, being mostly local produce. When it began, Legs Lemon would be sent off round the countryside collecting lorry-loads of apples which were picked by the locals, or by Tiddler's own 'boys,' at the height of the season.

In the root season, Tiddler also obtained his roots and plants from a supplier in Crowborough, Sussex. Legs Lemon would drive one of Tiddler Knowles' two vehicles, an Austin 7 tonner. This would be fully loaded with empty tins and orange

boxes, to fill with plants such as aster, lobelia, antirrhinum, carnation, petunia, salvia and alyssum. The journeys through the countryside, in the 1950s, were pretty slow. There were no motorways and lorries were usually packed to full capacity, making them very heavy and thus making the trips even slower. Time was always against the market trader in the earlier years, with produce deteriorating in lengthy tasks such as picking, packing and delivering. Everything took time and there were no modern machines to facilitate the processes.

During the Second World War, Tiddler kept his many countryside contacts and still purchased in bulk - enough to supply and allocate to his customers. Bananas, which were a rarity during the war, were the only commodity he preferred to sell from his own stall in Surrey Street. He was very generous to his farmer suppliers at Christmas time. Legs Lemon would deliver boxes of whisky, legs of pork, chicken, grapefruit, oranges and bananas, for their Christmas 'bonus.' Like Agnes, Tiddler didn't believe in banks, and hid all his cash away at home. Unlike Agnes, he kept all his in one place, in a jardinière which stood on his landing and was full of £500 bundles. A robbery took place in his house, one day, whilst he was absent. Even though the place was turned upside-down by the thieves, they never found any money.

Like the Lovett family, he also had connections, near Brighton, for wood purchases. The land had already been 'stripped,' and the wood, ready for collection, was brought back to Tiddler's yard for sawing into logs. This was just after the Second World War when it was virtually impossible to buy coal. This was called 'spare time work' by Tiddler Knowles.

As the years rolled by, Legs Lemon married and had his own family to support. Tiddler thought him still young, and single, and would telephone him saying: "Hello, son, I just want you to go and pick up those oranges from the docks, tomorrow morning, but you'll have to be there early," and Legs would sit up all night at the docks, worrying and waiting for the supplier. Or Tiddler Knowles would telephone and Legs Lemon would answer: "Hello, dad, what do you want now?" Tiddler would reply: "Hello, son, you know those apples you've just collected, early this morning, from Kent, well, I want you to take them, straight away, to the Portobello Road..." Finally Legs had had enough. After 23 years of working for Tiddler, on a daily, 24-hour 'call-out,' Legs decided it was really time to move on.

Legs decided to leave Tiddler, once and for all. He had actually quit six times, previously.

A few days later, Tiddler, in his mid-70s, died from a heart attack, whilst stacking boxes in his yard.

It was at this time that Legs Lemon acquired his own stall and traded along the same lines as Tiddler, keeping to what he knew. However, eventually he took a gamble and filled in with one or two other lines, such as tomatoes which he bought from Spitalfields and Covent Garden. These were locally-grown tomatoes which he preferred to sell unripe. He bought daily, as many as 150-200 boxes, and sold them off his stall and to local cafés and other stallholders. He, too, paid in cash, carrying as much as £250 to £300 some days.

Very few people would consider this safe, today, but for an individual, it was the only way to purchase stock. Because the tomato season was of short duration, he still kept to the roots and plants at the same time. His Christmas trade saw him taking another gamble and selling all types of nuts such as walnuts, almonds, chestnuts and hazelnuts. He would buy these about six weeks before Christmas, and spend as much as £1,000 on his Christmas stock. This was a line he gambled on, in the late 1960s, and one in which he was very successful.

Legs Lemon retired from Surrey Street in 1990, the place where he had been a familiar figure for 50 years.

"News, Star and Standard!"

Street characters

Goldie the newspaper man

Goldie was another 'roaming trader' and was quite a character, carrying his hessian sack full of papers and half-running, half-trotting. He went around the High Street, North End and Surrey Street, selling his newspapers and shouting: "News, Star and Standard, News, Star and Standard."

In addition to selling daily newspapers he was a vendor of special editions, new editions and racing results - horse racing being a favourite pastime in those days.

He was quite successful at his trade and was very convincing. He would shout out local headline news such as "Whale in Wandle," or report news of a house falling down in Thornton Heath, when in fact there may only have been a few roof tiles which had fallen to the street below. He would make everything into a national disaster and was warned, on several occasions, for his 'inaccuracies.'

My father believes he was fined the sum of 5s. (25p), by the local magistrates, on two or three occasions, for shouting out that war had been declared when it hadn't!

Goldie disappeared during the war and my father does not remember seeing him again, after that.

He wore a vest whatever the weather

The Phosferene Man

During the late 1930s the market extended into Frith Road, with less than a dozen stalls having pitches on the Debenhams' side.

As well as the permanent sites, a trader could purchase a licence for a casual pitch. One such casual was a chap named Joe Strong, the Phosferene Man. He used to sell five-inch high bottles of tonic called 'Phosferene,' a tonic which was supposed to give a person vitality and strength. One would imagine that Joe Strong was a regular user of his own tonic, judging from his well-built physique!

His pitch consisted of a board of plywood on two folding trestles, along with a punch-ball on a stand. The board became his demonstration table. To show off his super strength, and how it was improved by taking Phosferene, Joe would drive a six-inch nail halfway into the piece of plywood, with his hand, which was just wrapped in a rolled-up handkerchief or a tea towel. Ginger Thompson, who owned the '54 Café, in Surrey

Street, in the mid 1960s, recalled that along with this display, Joe would state: "In a minute I'll show you what my medicine does for you. I'll knock that punch-ball right over." He would then turn towards the punch-ball, show signs of throwing a punch at it, then turn back to his audience with more market spiel. Apparently he never did punch that ball.

My father remembers that Joe Strong always wore a singlet vest, so that he could display his muscular arms. This attire - or lack of it - he appeared to wear, whatever the weather.

Joe Strong came from London and pitched on a regular basis, weekends mainly. He had a brother who was more affluent than Joe. His brother dealt in cut price sets of china and teasets, dinner services and so on, which he used to auction outside the New Palladium in Surrey Street, and virtually opposite to Walter's stall.

My father believes that he has a descendant, Bob Strong, who still sells cut price china in some London markets today.

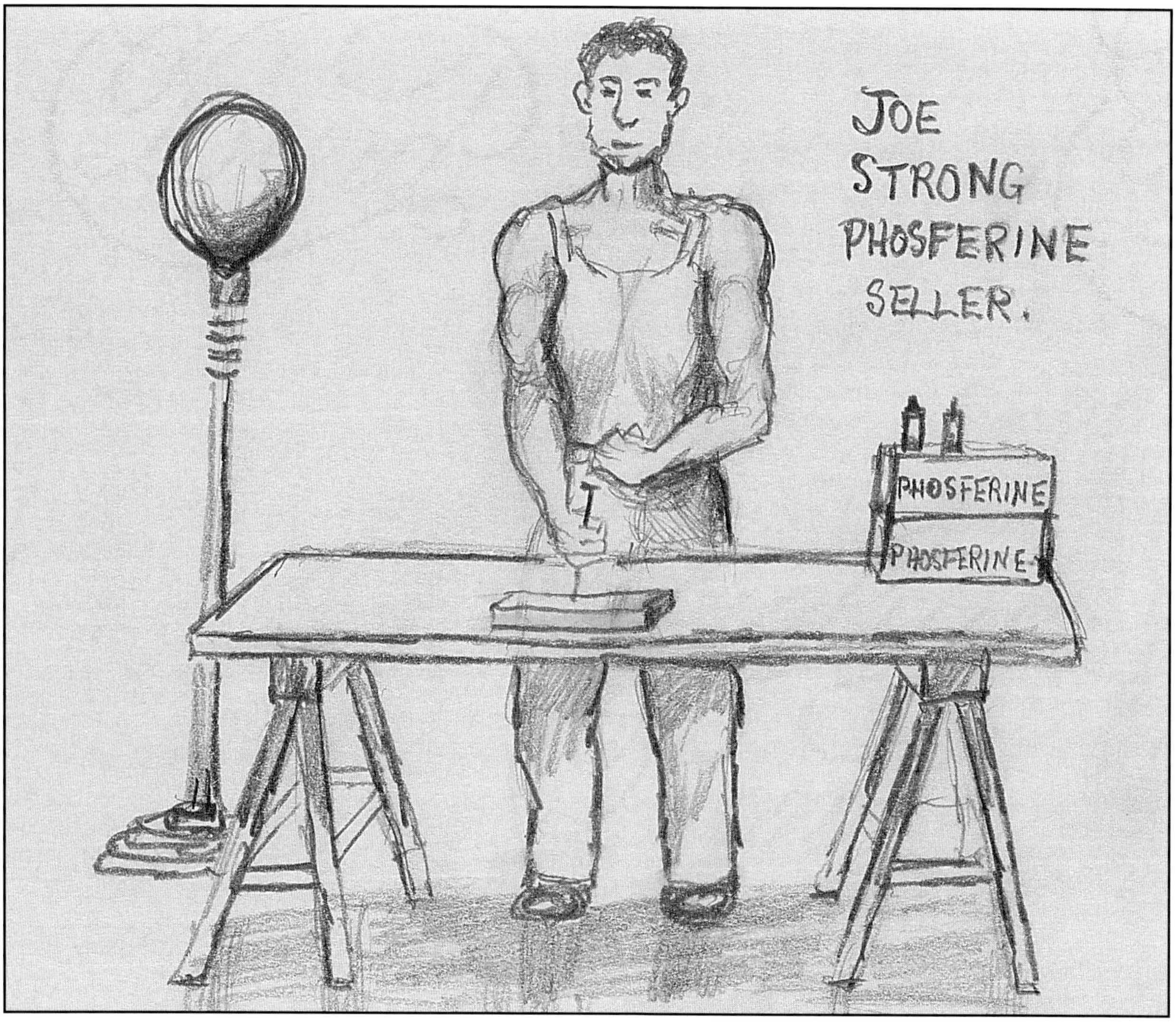

The one-toothed up-market down and out

Ol' Yates

Ol' Yates had been part of the Surrey Street scene for several decades. His home was in one of Walter's five stables in Church Path, where he had a warm and dry place to sleep each night.

He became invaluable to Walter, and the other street traders, by doing odd jobs for his 'beer money,' and could be found either digging the ground with other down-and-outs, on Walter's land in Mitcham, or taking the stalls to and from the various yards which were in the immediate vicinity, such as the Waterworks' Yard, Overton's Yard and one behind the jailhouse, to name but a few. When Croydon's biggest supermarket, Caters, opened in Surrey Street, in 1960, storage for many of the market traders became available beneath the store.

HARDWARE

—AND ALL GOODS FOR THE HOME

From the Supermarket Food Store you will see a brightly-lit wide staircase. Go up those stairs and let your eyes feast on this Aladdin's Cave of colourful and labour-saving implements for you, the 1960 housewife. Refrigerators, washing machines, spin-dryers, fires, glass, china, gifts, gardening equipment, in fact everything for the modern home. Bargains will be found by the hundred—and Christmas is only two months away.

THE STORE WITHIN A STORE

SPECIAL HIRE PURCHASE SCHEME

Items which are too heavy for the customer to carry home will be delivered in the Caters Supermarket van, and there is always our new credit scheme, which allows you 38 weeks to pay, or, of course, the normal hire purchase arrangements which place even the most expensive and luxurious goods within everybody's grasp.

THIS IS HOW you will come out of Caters Supermarket. Young ladies will take the money for all the goods you have purchased and others will pack them in the Caters carrier bags which are FREE.

OVEN-READY POULTRY

THERE will always be an abundant supply of our "Oven Ready" chickens with prices ranging, according to weight, from about 6s. to 14s. These chickens are reared on selected farms in the country and will be on sale in the Supermarket within a few days of being killed. "Oven Ready" means that the bird has already been cleaned and prepared so that all the housewife has to do is to place the bird in her oven and let it cook for the appropriate time.

HOT BARBECUE CHICKENS

Roasted on a spit

Perhaps the housewife hasn't got the time to cook the chicken herself. In that case, buy one of Caters specially cooked "Barbecue" chickens. These chickens are, as Arthur Askey would say, "Cooked before your very eyes," on Caters revolving spit. The customer receives the chicken in a foil-lined bag which retains the heat and, if placed in the oven in the bag for a few minutes, it will again be "piping hot."

At Caters Supermarket

CAR BOYS WILL BE AT YOUR SERV

When you visit the Supermarket by car on Friday evenings or Saturdays yo

avail yourself of Cater's 'CAR BOY SERVICE'

Their team of boys will be ready to carry your goods to yo

CATERS

opening

10 a.m.

TUESDAY

NEXT

Surrey Stree

Always Buy

WILKINSON'S

Pontefract Cake

MINT IMPERIALS | MINT SORTS

WILKO JAPS | LIQUORICE ALL-SORTS

WILKOMINTS | 4 oz. CARTONS 8d.

An advertisement from the *Croydon Advertiser* - 1960.

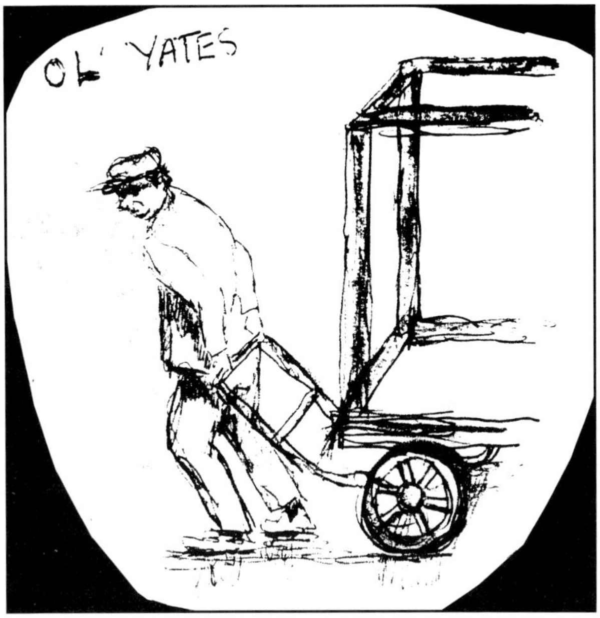

Ol' Yates with the stall.

Agnes ensured that Ol' Yates was a better-dressed down-and-out than most and supplied him with decent secondhand clothing which she bought at jumble sales. Although he wasn't allowed to cook in the stables he never went hungry. Agnes always made sure that he had a cooked meal each day.

Yates was a strange-looking man, with only one tooth, and it amazed my father as to its continued existence because Ol' Yates constantly wiggled his tooth with his tongue. He retained the tooth for many years and this was an asset when he was frightening away the local children from Walter's yard. Yates would only have to snarl and bare his tooth, for the tiny tots to flee.

Ol' Yates liked a drink and, because of this, a final visit by someone, to his stable, on the occasions when he staggered home, was vital, to ensure that all was safe. One evening my father ventured towards the stables, to hear Yates saying: "I'm going to put your lights out right this minute." My father became worried that someone else, a foe rather than a friend, was with Yates, so peeped through a crack in the stable door to see who was with him. But nobody was there, it was only Yates, with a lighted candle, which he was about to snuff out for the night!

CATERS SUPERMARKET

SURREY STREET, CROYDON — CROydon 6101 (6 lines)

MEAT

CANTERBURY LAMB CHOPS
LOIN CHOPS (trimmed) 3/- lb.
CUTLETS (trimmed) 2·4 lb.
Mixed Grills, Sweetbreads, Crown Lamb Roast, Saddle of Lamb

FRUIT & VEGETABLES

Manaos BRAZILS 3/- lb.
No. 1 Grade WALNUTS 2/- lb.
MIXED NUTS 2/6 lb.
CHINESE GOOSEBERRIES 4 for 1/-

FROZEN FOODS

GARDEN PEAS
Usually 1/11 1/5 Usually 1/- 9d.
Cream and Chocolate Sponges, Fish and Chips, Waffles, Roast Beef Dinner, Shrimps, Chicken Dinner, Prawns

HEALTH and BEAUTY
Large range of chemistry including
30 BRANDS OF SHAMPOOS

CONTINENTAL SECTION

KANGAROO TAIL SOUP
GREEN TURTLE SOUP
Large variety CHINESE FOODS
Continental Packet SOUPS and SEASONING
PICKLES, CURRIES, SPICES FROM INDIA
CUCUMBERS from Poland
GHERKINS from Hungary
Range of 14 PASTA SHAPES
CHESTNUT PUREE for Stuffing
RUM BUTTER
BRANDY BUTTER
HERRINGS in 9 varieties of Sauces
CONTINENTAL MUSTARDS

SHOP EARLY – SHOP IN COMFORT
IN
BRITAIN'S BIGGEST SUPERMARKET
WITH THE
LARGEST VARIETY OF FOODS AND HOUSEHOLD GOODS

CHINA and GLASS – KITCHEN GADGETS
CARPET SWEEPERS—BATHROOM FITTINGS

WASHING MACHINES
REFRIGERATORS
ELECTRIC FIRES
HEARTH FURNITURE

HARDWARE DEPT.
1st FLOOR

CREDIT TERMS—NO DEPOSIT
No Charge—38 weeks to pay

ELECTRIC LIGHT FITTINGS
ALL COOKING UTENSILS
CUTLERY
OIL HEATERS
1960 MODELS

OUR BARGAIN PRICES
SAVE YOU MONEY

FISH

COD FILLETS 2/- lb.
PLAICE 2/- lb.
HADDOCKS 2/- lb.
SMOKED ON THE PREMISES
Rainbow Trout, Oysters, Scampi, Lobsters, Bucklings, Mussels, Winkles, Crabs

PROVISIONS

CATERS FAMOUS CREAMY BUTTER, FRESH OR SALT 2/8 lb.
CANADIAN CHEDDAR 3/4 lb.
FINE FULL FLAVOUR

Finest DANISH BACON ONLY

Essex FARM EGGS
FROM OUR OWN PACKING STATIONS

CHICKENS
ENGLISH OVEN-READY
1/- off each bird

DELICATESSEN

Range of 12 SALAMIS
SAUSAGES from Turkey, Greece, Germany, Hungary, Switzerland
SALADS, Millionaires, Italian, Potato and Onion, Oriental Rice, Herring
60 varieties of Continental CHEESES
Continental BREAD and ROLLS
American COCKTAIL BISCUITS

An advertisement from the *Croydon Advertiser*, published just before Christmas, 1960.

Saturday visits in a maroon-coloured van

Sarsaparilla man

All one needed was fourpence a glass for Sarsaparilla to 'purify your blood.'

Come Saturday mornings the Sarsaparilla man would arrive in Surrey Street and park his van south of the old jailhouse, near the corner of Scarbrook Hill.

He was a casual trader, of Italian origin, who would arrive in a tanker-type van filled with this non-alcoholic, dark-coloured, cherry-flavoured cordial drink.

The van was highly decorative and was very eye-catching, painted maroon and with gold scroll-work around the edges of the vehicle. At the back of the tanker was a tap, with a bucket underneath, for catching the drips when pouring.

There was another bucket filled with water, left beside the van, which was used for washing up the glasses. On the side of the tanker was a narrow shelf which allowed the customer space to stand his glass.

The Sarsaparilla sold for 4d. (about 2p) per glass. The drink was made from dried roots of a climbing plant, indigenous to tropical America, and was formerly used in medicine to treat psoriasis, so it was probably sold as a tonic or 'health' drink.

Anyone keen to taste this drink, and while so-doing let their mind drift back to the Sarsaparilla Man of the 1930s and 1940s, should know that it is still available in Cockneys pie and mash shop, in Church Street, Croydon.

Many who have tried it report back that it is a very pleasant drink.

The Sarsaparilla Man was quite popular and came for many years to Surrey Street but, like so many other casual traders, disappeared with time.

END HALL - CROYDON
ESDAY, NOV. 23RD 1938 AT 8.15
K HAMBOURG
D FAMOUS PIANIST
BLÜTHNER PIANO
DOORS OPEN 7.30 P.M.
HALL
YDON
SNOW
IDEN
YDON
SOCIETY
DAY, SATURDAY
NOVEMBER, 1938
CROYDON AMATEUR BOXING
BOXING
CENTRAL BATHS HALL
WEDNESDAY NOV

Ninety stalls with diverse products

Surrey Street snippets

There are approximately 90 stalls in Surrey Street. Some of the stallholders are pictured on the following pages, with their stalls, illustrating the diversity of market trading and characters found there.

Mary Ann Attrell, pictured on facing page, and her husband, Jim (whose retinue is pictured above), had a pitch next to Walter's stall. They did not have a stall as such but a four-wheeled pony cart. When the pony was released the shafts would be pointed skyward, chained to the cart, which provided a ready-made stall, with the plants contained thereon. No packing out or packing up to do! My father said they looked a charming sight with their little dog, Jimmy, which sat on the pony's back when going to and from their yard in West Croydon c.1938.

John Powis, whose slogan is "tomatoes a speciality," is a member of another old and well-established trading family and one which is noted for finest quality salads. Try their wonderful home-cooked beet-root!

James Finch, above left, started a sweet stall in 1994, when he was 19 years old. Peter Hewitt, top right, is a regular shopper and owns one of the oldest family shops in Church Street. Below, left, Pennie Buxton is seen working on Pammy Locke's card stall and below, right, is Gordon Ashley, who sells underwear and socks on his stall.

Top left, Michael Curd, whose family is recalled in The fruit merchant chapter (p.61) and top right, is Jane Masters, who started her fashion stall in 1994. Bottom left, Wayne Turner, who became a stallholder in late 1994, sells bread and cakes and bottom right is Howard Leyser, who set up his fabric stall in 1992.

Paula Williams on her mother's jewellery and fashion stall.

Micky White, left, runs his Afro/Caribbean stall, with the help of Clint Minchella, right. Micky's sister, Cathy, runs the spice and herb stall opposite to him.

What would the market traders do without the help of this dustman, Dave Street?

Yvonne and Dennis White are helping out on their daughter, Cathy's, stall, where herbs and spices are sold. The Whites are an old-established trading family.

Zulifzuar Ali has been operating his linen stall since 1993.

Michael Wren started working in the market 40 years ago, when he was only seven years old.

'Soapy' Paul, left, a market character, has helped the traders load and pack up their stalls for more than 15 years.

Below, left, is a picture of Terry Ingram, who has been working in Surrey Street for around 16 years.

Dolly Brooks, below, right, has been a stall-holder for more than 45 years. The other traders, and customers, find her rhyming sales tickets amusing, especially those on her Bramley apples, which usually say: "Eat, bake, boil or fry, Make a pudding or a pie!"

Sunday was still a rest day, for stall-holders in Surrey Street, in the 1990s.

Prince Monolulu before Croydon magistrates

A BRIGHT, feathered head-dress in one hand and a shooting stick-parasol in the other, Ras Prince Monolulu, tipster extraordinary, strode regally into the dock at Croydon Magistrates' Court on Christmas Eve. This 79-year-old man, who is known on race courses all over Europe, was accused of insulting behaviour at Surrey Street, Croydon, the previous day. Monolulu, who lives at Cleveland Street, London, W.1., stoutly denied the charge. "Not guilty," he said, and his lucky charms jangled a chorus.

P-con. Patrick Mortimer told the court that he saw Monolulu grab shoppers by the arms and thrust racing pamphlets under their noses.

"A number of women had to shake themselves free of him," said P-con. Mortimer.

When he was arrested, Monolulu told the officer: "I can give you a couple of tips for Kempton Park."

From the dock, Monolulu protested to the magistrates: "This is just a waste of time, your lordships. I have been 40 years all over Europe, and I have never insulted anybody. I certainly never insulted a woman. I married six of them and I never insult them - it doesn't pay."

He said he went to Surrey Street to wish the stallholders a merry Christmas.

They were shaking his hand and asking about "the horse which was still running."

Brandishing his racing pamphlets, Monolulu declared: "I am doing work of national importance." Then he chanted: "Black man, for luck, white man for pluck."

The magistrates found the case proved. "There was a certain amount of annoyance caused," commented Mr. F.S. Parsons, presiding magistrate. Turning to Monolulu, he added: "In future you just be very careful how you..." "...Shake people's hands?" asked Monolulu.

Monolulu was discharged, conditionally, on payment of 4s. costs.

"Thank you, sir, Merry Christmas, and I will never come back here for a long time."

Then Monolulu smiled and said: "A gentleman gave me £1 to pay the fine, so I am O.K."

From the *Croydon Advertiser* of January 1st 1960.

The boxing fraternity

Surrey Street champions

Mark Hart and Don Cockell in action in the ring on October 17th 1950. This contest was for the British Light Heavyweight Championship.

Gilbert Allnutt's book *Boxing Was My Sport - Tom Fisher,* tells the story of Croydon boxers from the 1920s onwards, and is a valuable source of information concerning the town's link with this sport.

Croydon became well-known, and popular, in the boxing world from around the 1920s and '30s, and remains so today. The history of boxing in Croydon has been meticulously documented in Gilbert Allnutt's work and the author has kindly permitted some of the highlights to be recorded here, as well as allowing the use of some treasured photographs.

There were many gymnasiums locally, one of the first being the Acacias Hall, Pitlake, Croydon, which operated in the early 1900s. The mid - 1930s saw Surrey Street with a gymnasium which Charlie Bint and Alf Bliss managed. This gym was located behind Beano's music store, next to the Dog and Bull. The Gun, in Church Street, Croydon, was another - this was opened about 1944, when the Gloucester Road gymnasium was destroyed by bombs. Tom Fisher had been a professional boxer, manager and promoter, to name only a few of his accomplishments, and he ran The Gun gym in the 1940s. This gym saw talented boxers, such as Mark Hart, Albert Finch, Ron Pudney and others, in contests there.

Some boxers, in particular, were directly linked with the market. Mark Hart's and John Toohig's families have stalls in Surrey Street and in earlier years Albert Finch's father made and supplied stalls which, in those early days were mostly hired, for market traders in Surrey Street.

Mark Hart won an Amateur Boxing Association title in 1944, as a heavyweight. He turned professional in 1945 when he made his début at the Queensbury Club, in Soho. He fought Albert Finch on three occasions, the first two of these fights taking place at the Grand Theatre, in Clapham. The two were well-known to each other because they both trained at The Gun.

On one occasion Mark Hart out-pointed Albert Finch over 12 rounds. A return match took place at the Manor Place Baths, in Walworth, for the Southern Area Middleweight Championship, and Mark narrowly won.

Mark, then the Southern Middleweight Champion, met the undefeated Randolph Turpin on two occasions. Randolph was an aggressive fighter who had great force behind his punches. The first fight was won by Randolph, on points, the second was a draw. Randolph's older brother, Dick, an under-rated fighter at the time, was also a contender for the British Middleweight Championship title. Although he was a somewhat cautious fighter, he was cool and skillful. Dick fought Mark, and won on points. Other bouts followed for Mark, however, with a third meeting with Albert Finch. The venue was to be the Davis Theatre, Croydon. By this time Albert Finch had beaten Randolph Turpin and was on top form. Albert won the fight.

Having lost the Southern Middleweight Championship, Mark Hart fought cruiserweight, his opponent being Don Cockell, who won this particular fight and another, against Mark, at Haringey. Don Cockell was to become a deputy manager at the Royal Oak public house, in Surrey Street, when he retired from boxing.

Mark decided to retire from boxing, following this defeat by Don Cockell, and turned to refereeing, but after a while he missed the ring and made a come-back. He made some progress but decided to retire from boxing in the 1950s. To quote from Gilbert Allnutt's book: "Mark fought for the British title and two eliminators, held the Southern Area title at two weights and was a credit to British boxing."

Albert Finch was another local man who boxed at a professional show at the Acacias Hall. He trained at The Gun and entered many boxing arenas both at home and in Europe. Many of his later bouts were televised. Albert also turned professional, in 1945, making his début at the Queensbury Club, just as Mark had done. His first fight resulted in a draw but he went on to gain 13 wins following this contest. Albert found that 1948 started badly for him; an old injury to his left hand gave him trouble and an abscess had formed on his right hand, which had put him out of action in the latter part of 1947. He topped the bill at the Royal Albert Hall, in London, one of the most prestigious venues in this country. This was in April 1948, with the undefeated Randolph Turpin. It was a points win for Albert. He continued with various wins around the country and

Albert Finch, the Middleweight Champion of Great Britain, pictured on April 24th 1950.

Jim Toohig, c.1936.

had his third bout with Mark Hart, at Croydon, which resulted in his first victory over him.

In 1949, he fought Dick Turpin, for the British Middleweight Championship. Although he lost this fight he had done well enough to warrant a return match with Dick Turpin, for the British and Empire Middleweight Championship, at Nottingham Ice Rink, which carried on for 15 rounds. Albert worked hard in this particular fight, and the reward was his. At long last Croydon had a champion.

It was in 1951 that Albert returned as a light heavyweight, unsuccessfully attempting to take two more British titles. Albert was to retire in 1958 but continued to live for many years in Croydon and regularly visited Surrey Street.

Jim Toohig was classed as a welterweight, in the 1930s, and the Acacias Hall, in Pitlake, would always have a full house if he was billed. The Acacias Hall and Mitcham Baths were the venues of many wins for Jim in the '30s. There was an occasion in 1933, at the Royston Hall, Penge, when all three brothers, Jim, John and Billy, appeared on the same programme.

Jim Toohig was put in the national top ten ratings, when a fight against Dixie Cullen in 1934 at Streatham Arena ended in a draw. He continued in good style, with various wins, for many years, and to quote again from Gilbert Allnutt's book: "Jim had a record to be proud of, and was one of Croydon's pre-war greats."

Surrey Street traders are great supporters of boxing and their local boxers. The boxing fraternity can usually be found in Surrey Street. In the 1930s, former Croydon bantamweight, Albert Jeal, ran his gym on the site of the fire station, in Old Town.

In addition to Tom Fisher's and Alf Bliss's gyms, there was another in Croydon, run by Ernie Brimble. The trainer of the boxers, in Ernie's gym, was Alf Bastin, who worked in Surrey Street.

After the launch of *Boxing Was My Sport*, in October 1976, Alf, and other Croydon ex-boxers, joined the London Ex-Boxers Association. The group published a magazine called *Box On,* which was sold in Surrey Street, by Alf Bastin, with the same enthusiasm, and success, as he had shown when selling cauliflowers from the stall. Alf introduced Gilbert Allnutt to Dicky Martin, a popular flyweight during the pre-war period, and to Bill Curd, a prominent stallholder, who, in the post-war period was an Inspector of the British Boxing Board of Control, and a familiar figure at the ringside of boxing shows in London.

Then they met the Gillams, a real boxing family of stallholders. Johnny Gillam, snr. was a popular, and most talented, amateur boxer. Gilbert remembers his contests with local boxer, Ted Giles, at the Applegarth Club, Thornton Heath, which took place in the late 1920s. In the mid-'30s, in addition to Bliss's gym, in Surrey Street, there were gyms run by Tom Fisher, Albert Jeal, Ernie Brimble and amateur units run by the Croydon Amateur Boxing Club as well as the Applegarth Club in Heath Road, Thornton Heath.

Alf Bliss's Surrey Street gym, which he and

CROYDON BOXERS IN TOP CLASS

Big-fight memories of Hart and Finch

CROYDON for years had a reputation for producing fighters—or boxers, as the men of the fistic trade are more politely known to-day. Croydon in its time has provided leading men at all weights and has raised at least one British champion in the professional ranks.

At the present time, Croydon cannot lay claim to, possessing any great stars of the Ring, but before long there may arise again new talent, men whose names will be known from one end of the country to the other. Who knows? **(writes "RINGSIDER".)**

A century or more ago, Croydon was known as a centre for prizefighting and the "Fancy" would travel from miles around to see the bloody bare-fist battles at Duppas Hill, Mitcham Common and other spots.

PRIZEFIGHT DAYS

When prizefighting was declared illegal, secret venues had to be arranged and the fights would be held soon after dawn at some remote spot known only to the contestants and their followers.

Even so, news of a prize-fight would sometimes leak out to the Parish Beadles and the Police and more than once the pugilists and their seconds finished the day behind bars in the old Croydon jail in Surrey-street.

Croydon saw its last bare-fist professional fight about 80-odd years ago and to dodge the watchful eyes of the police, the contestants and their handlers were taken in a large horse-drawn van to a spot somewhere near the Waddon Marshes.

The fight had lasted more than 20 rounds when a man posted as a look-out shouted, "Police!" The bruised and blood-covered fighters were hustled back into

some of the best men in Europe and who might have become a champion if he had been handled by the right people of the day.

Indeed, he did fight men of championship class such as Bugler Lake (against whom he went 17 rounds at the old Crystal Palace, despite the fact that he had been brought in as a last minute substitute) and often he had to give weight away to heavier opponents in order to obtain contests.

The names of many other fine Croydon boys who followed Jeal come readily to mind (many of them were trained by Jeal). We think of Jim Toohig, who fought Dave McCleave who went on to win the British welter-weight title. His brother Johnny Toohig, Tom Fisher, Charlie Bint, Herbie Spencer, Harry Barnes, Jack Greenslade, Marvin Hart and a host of others were all men to be reckoned with inside the roped square.

And let me say here that for more than 30 years, most of the Croydon boxers have owed a lot to the help and encouragement of veteran promoter, Mr. Bill Goodwin. Without Bill Goodwin, Croydon would never have gained the place on the fistic map that it did.

There was Eddie Steele, the South Norwood heavyweight, who beat Tommy Farr and fought great contests with men like Walter Neusel, the then German champion.

was much too good for most of the men in the 12 st. 7 lb. division and had to seek opponents among the heavyweights—an occupation that pleased Sid plenty.

He used to say, "I like nothing better than a really big heavyweight. The bigger they come, the better I like 'em".

Although his best fighting weight was round 13 st., Hart carried the punch of a 15 st. man and he knocked out a succession of heavyweights—British, Continental and Canadian—well inside the distance.

A great puncher, too, was the other man with the same name, Mark Hart, who rose to the top after the war. Never did Croydon produce a boy of greater courage than Mark, for he fought not only tough top-class opponents, but weight troubles as well.

AMATEUR HEAVYWEIGHT

Winning the British amateur heavyweight championship during the war while serving in the R.A.F., he turned professional after the end of hostilities, but his professional advisers decided that he was not tall enough to remain a heavyweight and they set about training him down to 11 st. 6-lb. to fight as a middleweight. Mark lost the weight and, unfortunately, he lost a lot of his punching power, too.

He won many grand scraps; he was beaten, too, but never disgraced. But once he joined the ranks of the "middles", that devastating left hook which had flattened men of 14 or 15 stones in his amateur days, was seldom seen again.

RISE OF ALBERT FINCH

In August 1945, a stylish and skilful amateur middleweight boxer turned to the professional game. His name? Albert Finch, who was soon to become the pride of Croydon and the only

Taken from a *Times and County Mail* supplement, June 10th 1960.

boxer, Charlie Bint, ran, was opened to be a training gym for Alf's discovery, Sid Hart, who became a long-standing resident in Croydon and who was well-known, for years, to the market's boxing men. Although not related to Mark Hart, under Alf Bliss's management he looked destined to challenge for a southern area light heavyweight championship.

In February 1982 the Croydon Ex-Boxers Association was formed. Its objectives were to provide a meeting place, in the Croydon area, for ex-boxers and boxing supporters, to give financial and other aid to ex-boxers and, at the committee's discretion, to charitable organizations, too. Sadly, Alf Bastin died in the spring of 1981, but right up to the time of his death, he was still training young men in 'The Noble Art.'

Therefore the association came too late for him, but his name is recalled, by its members, with great affection. Jim Toohig and Albert Finch accepted vice-presidencies and later, Mark Hart, on his return from living in Spain, was elected to the committee and later became a vice-president.

Vic Bowyer, an outstanding amateur boxer in the 1960s, and a familiar face in Surrey Street, joined the association and other members included Billy Chamberlain, who trained at The Gun gymnasium; Alf Bliss and Bill Goddard, who assisted Tom Fisher at both The Russell and The Gun gyms.

At the inaugural meeting, Alf Bliss accepted the post of assistant secretary and volunteered to be the welfare visitor.

He served the association with enthusiasm and hard work and attended a London meeting just two days before his death, at the age of 82, in January 1995.

He left a widow, Lily, who had also once worked in Surrey Street, at her father's stall. Ginger Thompson, with strong Surrey Street connections, took over the welfare visiting previously carried out by the late Alf Bliss.

The Croydon Ex-Boxers Association was able to help John Toohig to obtain sheltered housing and, thanks to the Croydon Council's Housing Department, was later able to re-house three other members in sheltered homes.

The charitable causes supported by the association were mainly Croydon-based and included the Mayday Hospital Scanner Appeal, the Friends of Mayday Hospital, the Crosfields mini-Olympics team, the Whitehorse Manor School War Memorial Restoration Fund and the Saint Christopher Hospice, Sydenham.

Bill Curd worked tirelessly, keeping a link between Surrey Street traders and the Croydon Ex-Boxers Association. He organized darts matches between the ex-boxers and the traders, for the Jim Toohig Trophy, with the proceeds going to the association's charitable fund.

Twice a year the association has published a nostalgic magazine, bought by around 30 stallholders, and the support and interest of Lord Weatherill of Croydon, a life-member of the Croydon Ex-Boxers Association, whose father was a boxer and wrestler, has proved invaluable.

The link between the Surrey Street traders and the Ex-Boxers Association continues to flourish to the present day.

The federation chairman

Mr. Croydon

John Williams, standing close to his haberdashery stall in Surrey Street, in 1994.

It becomes evident, as this chapter is read, just why John Williams has been dubbed "Mr. Croydon." I believe that he has done more for Surrey Street and the market traders, than any other individual.

Stallholders are a varied bunch, who come from all walks of life and have different reasons for trading in the market place. There is a stigma attached to a market trader, even today, and it is to be hoped that this book will enlighten the reader, so that he, or she, can appreciate that not all stallholders are 'Del-boy' types. John Williams most certainly is not.

He was born in West Croydon, in 1944. On leaving school John was employed in a variety of occupations, from shop work to selling his own goods, such as pens and dusters, from a suitcase on street corners. By the age of 19 he ventured on to the street market scene and by 1969 he had acquired a permanent pitch in Surrey Street. By this time he was selling haberdashery, something he has continued to do ever since. At one point he also ran a shop at 49, Surrey Street, now the main headquarters of the Surrey Street Federation. He was in partnership with his brother, Tony, and they developed quite an empire in their heyday, with stalls in Surrey Street and Kingston as well as trading at several one-day markets.

The birth of the recent Surrey Street Traders'

John Williams' haberdashery stall, at the end of a 'perfect' and great day, in November 1994.

Federation grew out of the pedestrianization of North End. Traders were concerned about the removal of their shoppers' transport from North End, which had many of the best 'bus routes, so a petition was raised which helped delay the pedestrianization by a couple of years. Michael Wren, the 'eggman,' and John Williams, were the driving force behind the petition and the traders then asked the pair to form a federation. This took place in 1988 and they set about trying to improve working conditions for the traders, to improve relationships with the council and other local bodies and to enhance conditions and amenities for shoppers.

Subscriptions from the stallholders enabled the federation to support charities and promote the market. Their shopping list included Christmas lights (bought on a cost-sharing basis with the council), and buying hanging baskets for the street. They have taken part in the Croydon Carnival every year, winning the Best Float category on two occasions.

The federation has supported many charities, both local and national, including the Homeless of Croydon, Cancer Research, Leukaemia Research and the British Heart Foundation.

The federation is a branch of the National Market Traders' Federation, which has about 40,000 members, and negotiates with Croydon Council on all market matters. It supports and represents all members at Town Hall meetings, discussing with the council about the 'trades facility' in Surrey Street car park. It also gives each Mayor of Croydon a guided tour of the market, complete with lunch and entertainment, and talks to customers should any ever have problems. Involvement includes monitoring the level of street cleaning, rubbish clearance, and ensuring that the council runs the market correctly. Basically, it is a union, and is there to promote Surrey Street, Croydon and the federation, in that order.

John Williams believes that the market place is a very traditional one and that it needs to be preserved, rather than changed. Surrey Street is a special place, not only because of its long history but, more importantly, because of the people working there. They form a community which has many characters. John's is an ideal voice for the market trader, Surrey Street, and Croydon as a whole. His rôle is well-suited because he is the President of the Croydon Speakers' Club, and relishes addressing the public. He frequently gives talks on the history of Surrey Street market and on Croydon in general.

The Royal visit to Surrey Street market, by His Royal Highness the Prince of Wales, on November 29th 1994, was John's idea. He wrote a number of letters telling Prince Charles about the history of the market, the characters it contained and the traditions which they uphold.

John Williams also mentioned that the market was rather like the Monarchy: "...old fashioned and in decline!" Local arrangements for the visit included liaison with the police and with the fire service, who also helped by putting up the street bunting. The whole street took three weeks to dress, for the visit, and that included working on Sundays.

On the great day each stallholder had dressed his or her own stall, with pictures of Prince Charles and messages such as "We love you, Charles," on posters. John knew exactly when the Prince would be arriving, by using a two-way radio. Everything was timed perfectly. Prince Charles met the Leader of the Council, Mary Walker, the Mayor, Councillor Wally Garrett, and when he finally approached John, the Prince joked: "Ah, so you're the man I've got to blame for all this!"

The Surrey Street scene was a sea of smiling faces, people clapping, others waving flags, all cheering and shouting. The Lovett's stall was the first to be introduced to Prince Charles, because it was the oldest trading in Surrey Street.

John also introduced the Prince to the four generations of the Dyer family - including great-grandson, Jack jnr. who was only three weeks old. The Prince met many of the best-loved characters, including Jack and Pat Hogg, known affectionately as 'Mr. and Mrs. Surrey Street,' 'John the singing fishmonger' and 'Jellied Eel George.'

John Williams handed Prince Charles his presentation, a personal letter, and mentioned that it had taken nearly 800 years for the market to have a Royal visitor, but it had certainly been worth the wait.

The Prince's visit was one of the high spots of John's market life. He remarked that Prince Charles was very easy to talk to, saying that he really is "The People's Prince."

A few days later John received a letter of thanks from Prince Charles' Private Secretary, informing him that the Prince had had a wonderful time and that he would write to him personally, which he later did. It was the perfect ending to a perfect visit - except that it is not an ending but a beginning. John said he felt sure that there is now a bond between the Prince and the Surrey Street market. You only have to look at the photographs which follow, and read the foreword to this book to know that the Prince genuinely cares.

The Royal visit

It may look like a thriving market, but business came to a standstill on the day of the visit.

Photograph courtesy of the Picture Partnership,

The Prince chats to helper Andy Jackson, who works on Marvin Thorogood's (The Banana King's) stall.

Photograph courtesy of the Picture Partnership, Croydon.

A thoughtful moment for the Heir to the Throne, as he listens to Zulifzuar Ali, who runs the linen stall. John Williams, Surrey Street Federation chairman, is to the Prince's left.

Photograph courtesy of the Picture Partnership, Croydon.

Almost everyone looked up at the buildings as office workers shouted: "Charles, Charles!" and waved to the Prince, who waved back to them.

Photograph courtesy of the Picture Partnership, Croydon.

More office workers catch the Prince's attention.

Photograph courtesy of the Picture Partnership, Croydon.

The Prince looks in at the stall of John Birch, the 'singing fishmonger.'

Photograph courtesy of the Picture Partnership, Croydon.

A shopper catches the Prince's attention.

Photograph courtesy of the Picture Partnership, Croydon.

So many hands to shake.
Photograph courtesy of the Picture Partnership, Croydon.

Prince Charles enjoys life 'on the other side' at Croydon's oldest public house, the Dog and Bull, in Surrey Street.

Picture reproduced by kind permission of the Croydon Advertiser *Group Limited.*
Photographers: Kevin Shaw and Nick ffrench.

A day to remember, as stallholder Gary Dickson awaits a Royal handshake.

Picture reproduced by kind permission of the Croydon Advertiser *Group Limited.*
Photographers: Kevin Shaw and Nick ffrench.

The Prince meets three generations of the Dyer family: Darren, 'Big John,' and baby, Jack jnr.

Picture reproduced by kind permission of the Croydon Advertiser *Group Limited.*
Photographers: Kevin Shaw and Nick ffrench.

A stop for a quick snack at Jellied Eel George's seafood stall.

Picture reproduced by kind permission of the Croydon Advertiser *Group Limited.*
Photographers: Kevin Shaw and Nick ffrench.

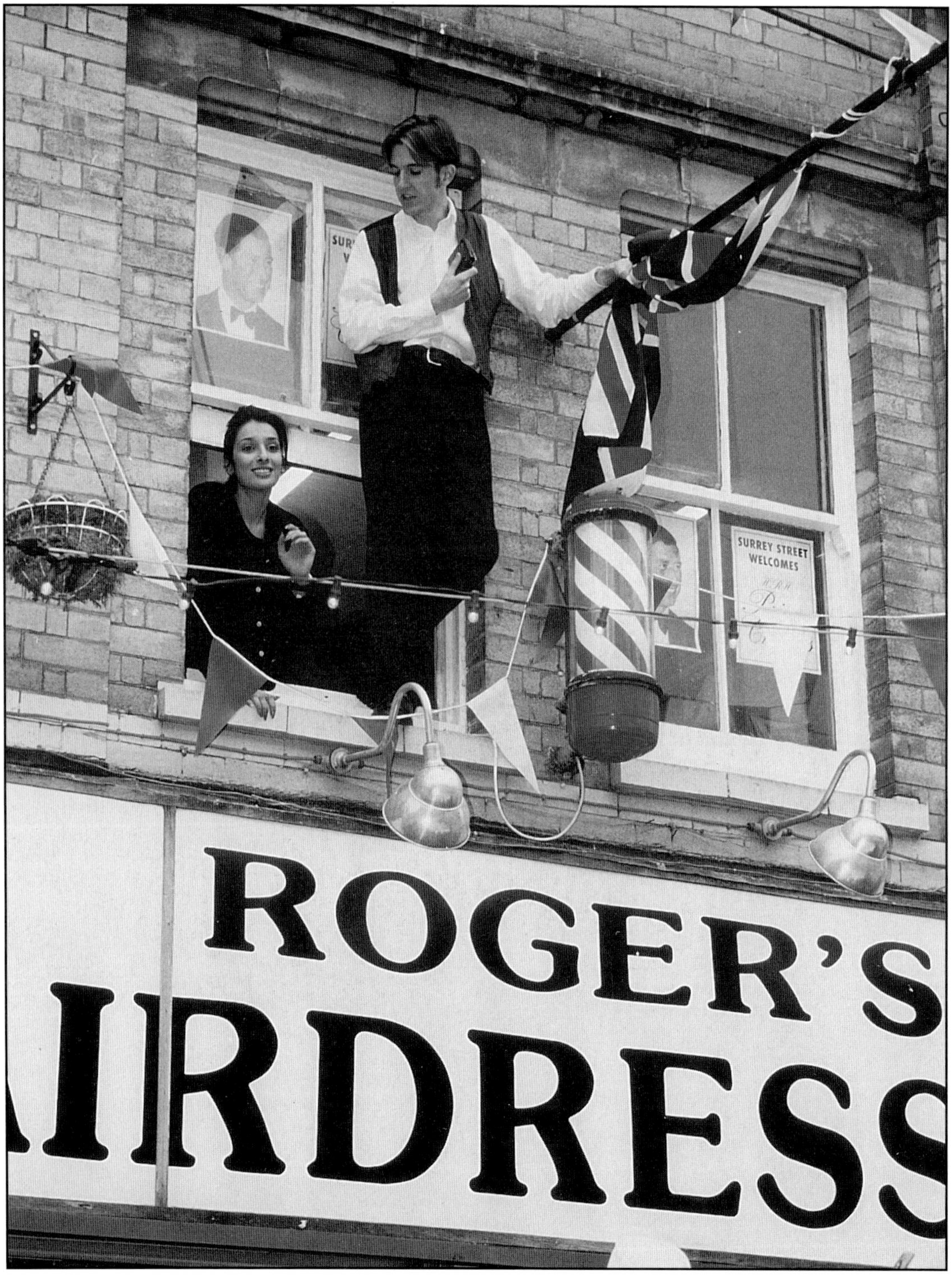

Employee Paris Yukon gives Sophie Khan a running commentary, whilst viewing the Royal visit from a hair-raising vantage point!

Picture reproduced by kind permission of the Croydon Advertiser *Group Limited.*
Photographers: Kevin Shaw and Nick ffrench.

Awaiting a visit from the Prince is the Gillam family. The youngest member is Alesha, seen here with her mother, Marie, and grandmother, Kathy.

Picture reproduced by kind permission of the Croydon Advertiser *Group Limited.*
Photographers: Kevin Shaw and Nick ffrench.

'Big John' Dixon, who has a vegetable stall, enjoyed one of the Prince's remarks: "He told me he admired the size of my carrots!"

Picture reproduced by kind permission of the Croydon Advertiser *Group Limited.*
Photographers: Kevin Shaw and Nick ffrench.

Just one of the many handshakes by the Prince during the course of the visit.

Picture reproduced by kind permission of the Croydon Advertiser *Group Limited.*
Photographers: Kevin Shaw and Nick ffrench.

Jack and Pat Hogg ('Mr. and Mrs. Surrey Street') presented the Prince with a gigantic mushroom, adorned with a flower. When he shook the Prince's hand, Jack remarked: "I bet that's done a bit of mileage, hasn't it, Sir?"

Picture reproduced by kind permission of the Croydon Advertiser *Group Limited.*
Photographers: Kevin Shaw and Nick ffrench.

Prince Charles bids farewell to Surrey Street.
Photograph courtesy of the Picture Partnership, Croydon.

The market must be preserved

Epilogue

After the Second World War, street markets saw an influx of traders. Many were ex-servicemen, who, with few overheads, could try their luck in the market place. However, over the decades, with lessening poverty and improvements in education and career prospects, fewer and fewer stallholders, at least as far as Surrey Street is concerned, have encouraged their offspring to continue to work in the family businesses.

There's an air of despondency, an air of resignation, almost, amongst the traders in Surrey Street, and it all seems to be due to what is termed 'progress.' It threatens their very livelihood, in the form of competition from supermarkets, with their convenience foods, and garden centres, all of which have free parking.

There is a multi-storey car park right behind the Surrey Street market place but parking there is so expensive that some people will not use it. It is becoming increasingly difficult for the market trader, in general, to compete, and, in particular, Surrey Street is in neglect.

It reminds me of a plant which Walter bought Agnes just after the Second World War. It was a peace rose, a hybrid tea rose, specially propagated to commemorate the end of the war. Agnes nourished and tended this plant for a decade, then, the year she died the rose bush died, too. Agnes had been the one who nurtured the plant and it flourished under her caring hands, but once she passed away the rose was forgotten and so it withered and died.

Surrey Street is part of our heritage and, like other street markets, deserves preservation. It's a unique institution which is crumbling badly and needs support - especially financially - if it is to survive.

I hope my, albeit small, contribution, to our Croydon heritage, in relating stories about some of the Surrey Street market traders, will help to preserve a little of their history for young and old alike to enjoy, now and in the future. However, reading books, and glancing at glossy photographs, can only hint at past life. We can learn so much more from the original artefacts, buildings and architecture. As long as we continue to demolish and destroy these, our heritage, our sense and imagination of the past, can only be further dulled. Books, alone, are not enough. Croydon, in recent years, has destroyed its heritage with an excess of zeal. We are now, at least, fortunate in having a museum, Lifetimes, in Croydon, which opened in March 1995. If only one of our old Surrey Street buildings, such as the former jailhouse, could have been saved for posterity. What a museum that could have made, being right at the core of old Croydon!

Conservation is not a modern phenomenon. This is a newspaper report from the *Old and New Croydon Illustrated*, dated May 1894: "To a casual observer the architectural peculiarities of Surrey Street are summed up as being dirt and dilapidation, but careful inspection of many of the places will reveal, after the dirt has been removed, some really artistic work.

"If the old houses in Surrey Street, Croydon, had been as carefully, and constantly, plied with water and whitewash, the woodwork with paint and polish, as are those at Chester, then King Street, Middle Row, Market Street, would not have been relegated to oblivion and Surrey Street would be visited, annually, by thousands of American visitors."

Surrey Street market and buildings are at the heart of Croydon, and in the hearts of Croydonians. They must not be allowed to turn into a dilapidated disaster, just waiting to collapse in the cause of 'progress.'

I would like to envisage our market - yes, yours and mine - going through the 21st century with smart, up-graded listed buildings and all types of street trading, not just the fruit and veg., plant and flower stalls for which Surrey Street is renowned, but with antique and secondhand book stalls, china, jewellery stands and other diversities. All would enhance the prospects of regular customers and even tourism...

...so please remember what happened to my grandmother's Peace rose and don't let our market become Once Upon A Time.

About the author

VIVIEN Lovett was born in Croydon and now lives in Wallington, Surrey. She is married and has grown-up twin sons. Currently she is studying advanced piano-playing and intermediate level violin. She also teaches primary and junior children piano and music theory. Her hobbies include pen and ink sketching, reading true-life adventure stories, and participating in racing the family's 25ft. Hustler sailboat on the River Thames. She enjoys long walks with her dog, Zoe, as well as pottering in the garden - her favourite place.

ACKNOWLEDGEMENTS

I would dearly like to thank the following for their valued contributions, stories and photographs, towards Surrey Street, Croydon - a stall story*: Gilbert Allnutt (The boxing fraternity); Lily Bliss; Bill Curd (The fruit merchant); Mark and Rose Hart (The Harts); Wally Jackson - ex-eccentric dancer - (To be or not to be...a market trader); Mike Jarman (Jaffa Joe); Hew Lemon (Legs Lemon and Tiddler Knowles); Mrs. Pat Mitchelle (The big firm); Fred Redpath; Ginger Thompson; John Toohig snr. (The big firm); cousins Miriam and Linda Baharier (The toy stall); Betty Ball (The root man); Tessa Carter (The root man); my late uncle, Jack Garcia (The toy stall); cousin Maureen Golding (The root man); Uncle Bert and Aunt Olive Lovett (Firmly-established); my elder brother, David William Lovett jnr. (The Woodcote nurseryman); cousin, Ian, and his wife, Rosanna Lovett (Rose's garden) and cousin, Terry Smith (Stubbing up). My very special thanks to all of the following: my dear father, Bill Lovett, for so many of the detailed accounts, the pen and ink sketches and for the painting on the back cover; my wonderful husband, Les Whitehouse, for his continued support; John Williams, Surrey Street Federation Chairman, to whom I am indebted for his support and interest throughout this venture and my many thanks for his promotional work; the publishers, Frosted Earth, who laid a smooth path for me to tread;* Croydon Advertiser *Group Limited for the use of so many photographs, including several of the Royal visit, and for newspaper cuttings; Croydon Local Studies Library and Archives Service, for use of their material and photographs, and the team, especially Oliver Harris, Borough Archivist; the Picture Partnership for the use of several Royal Visit photographs; Sally Macdonald, Principal Museum Officer of the Croydon Libraries, Museums and Arts, who gave me encouragement to turn a family keepsake into a stall story; Jess Steele, Heritage Officer, London Borough of Croydon for her help and guidance and Croydon Snappy Snaps for their efficient service. Last, but not least, Derek Bradford, who, throughout, conveyed to me his cool, calm and collected thoughts when pondering the typescript. I do apologize, sincerely, if I have omitted any person or persons. This is quite unintentional. I also apologize for omitting many stories because of lack of space.* Sponsor: *Croydon Libraries Museum and Arts.*

PHOTOGRAPH CREDITS

In addition to the picture acknowledgements already given to *The Croydon Advertiser Group* and *The Picture Partnership* for the use of their Royal photographs, I would also like to thank the following: *The Croydon Advertiser* Group for Agnes Lovett (p.6); Agnes Lovett (p.24); Bill Lovett and painting (p.43); Bert, Agnes and Bill Lovett (p.45); Ian and Rosanna Lovett (p.49); Richard Dimbleby and Mark Hart (p.64); Jim Toohig (p.66); advertisements (pp. 72 to 73); news cutting (p.83); news cutting (p.87). *Croydon Local Studies Library* for Church Path (p.8); Agnes and Walter Lovett at stall (p.10); Walter's stalls in their heyday (p.31), Up the top end (p.47); The Old Jail House (p.60); Surrey Street Market Traders (p.62); Surrey Street, Croydon (p.68), Surrey Street in the 1960s (front cover), Ordnance Survey map, (p.4). *Fielding Photographs, Leeds*: Dorothy Lovett (p.17); *Holiday Snaps, Margate:* Walter Lovett (p.23); *H.Ward, Photographer, West Croydon:* Bill Lovett (p.26); *The Sheffield Photo Company:* Lion tamer photo (p.52); *U.S.A.Studios:* Betty Lovett (p.53); *O.P.S. Exclusive,* Will Hay (p.56); *The Topical Press Agency Ltd:* Hart and Cockell (p.84).

BIBLIOGRAPHY

A Pictorial History of Boxing, by Nat Fleischer and Sam Andrew
The Plant Hunters, by Charles Lyte
Boxing Was my Sport -Tom Fisher, by Gilbert Allnutt
Relics of Old Croydon, by John Ollis Pelton
History and Antiquities of Croydon, by the Rev. D.W. Garrow
Croydon in the Past. Historical, Monumental and Biographical, published by Jesse W. Ward, Croydon
Croydon. The Story of a Hundred Years, published by the Croydon Natural History and Scientific Society Ltd.
Old and New Croydon Illustrated, a *Croydon Advertiser* 'special.'